SURVIVING
ON HOPE

SURVIVING

ON

HOPE

A Memoir of the Holocaust and a Life Beyond

TOM NEWMAN

PAGE TWO

Cataloguing in publication information is available from Library and Archives Canada.
ISBN 978-1-77458-084-4 (paperback)
ISBN 978-1-77458-170-4 (ebook)

Page Two
pagetwo.com

Copyedited by Crissy Calhoun
Proofread by Alison Strobel
Cover and interior design by Jennifer Lum

TO MY BELOVED PARENTS,
*Rosalia and Alexander; brothers Isaac, Artur, and
Morris; and sisters Friderika, Ludmila, and Irena,
all of whom died in the darkness of the Holocaust.
You live on in my heart always.*

TO ALL OF MY GRANDPARENTS,
*aunts, uncles, and cousins.
May your memory be for a blessing.*

TO MY LOVING AND SUPPORTIVE FAMILY.
*Living with hope years ago, I could not have
imagined the wonderful family I would live to
create and be blessed with. I cherish my beautiful
daughters, Audrey and Alexandria; my son-in-law,
Graham; and my grandchildren, Blake, Cole,
Madison, Jared, and Harrison. And to Grace,
with whom I share such a beautiful life.
You all bring me true happiness.*

Hope is the one thing that helps sustain us to get through the darkest of times.

SURVIVING ON HOPE

FORMER NAZI CAMPS
ON THE POST-1945 MAP OF EUROPE

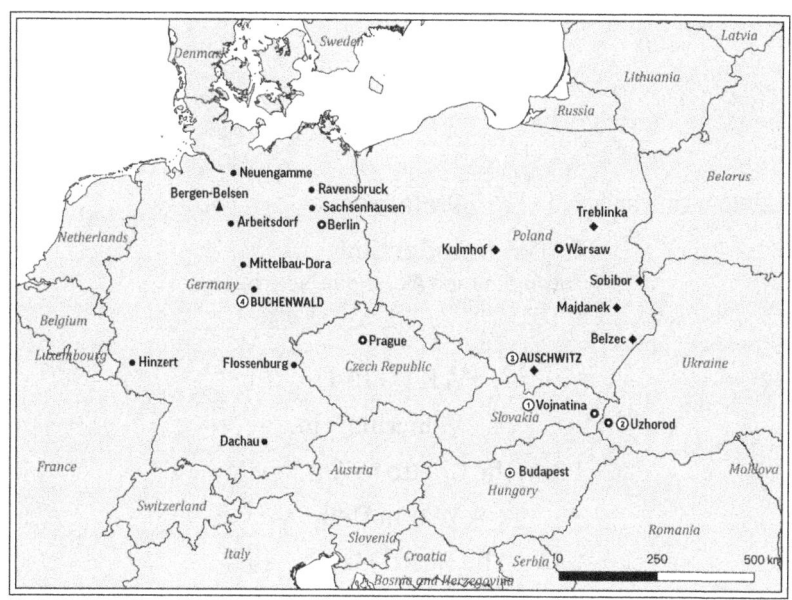

CAMP TYPE
- ◆ Extermination
- ● Slave labour
- ▲ Holding/Other

TOM'S JOURNEY DURING THE WAR
1 Vojnatina
2 Uzhorod
3 Auschwitz
4 Buchenwald

From broadstreet.blog/2020/10/19/quantitative-social-science-and-the-holocaust/. Thanks to Volha Charnysh for sharing the map of former Nazi camps on the post-1945 map of Europe.

CONTENTS

PART TWO

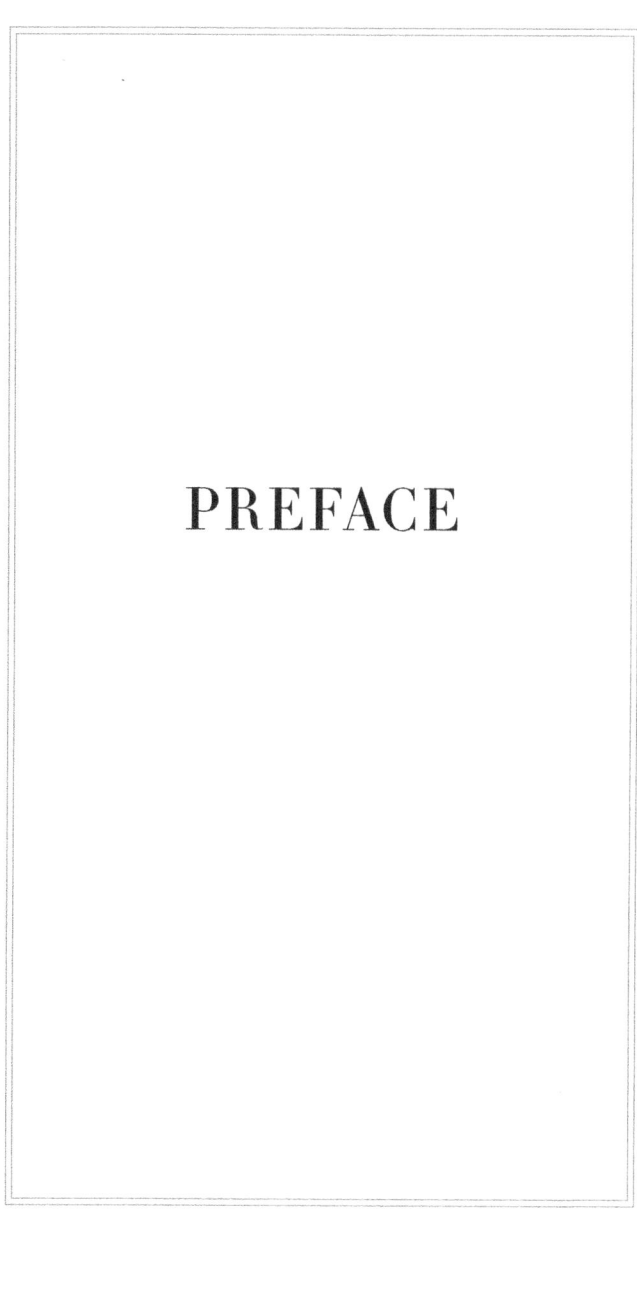

PREFACE

L IKE SO MANY who suffered untold brutalities in Nazi concentration camps, I spent most of the rest of my life suppressing it. The memories were too extreme and painful to relive. I did not talk about it much, and when I had children, I told them little about it. Although if they asked, I would provide a few carefully selected details. It is not that I believed they should not know about it; from time to time, I would direct them toward a film, such as *The Diary of Anne Frank*, or a documentary, or an article in a newspaper. I wanted my children to learn about the Holocaust and know what I went through without having to relive it myself. Further, a crime against humanity, such as the Holocaust, must never be forgotten.

In my effort to move on with my life, I had tried to bury those horrific memories. Ultimately, though, it is those who experienced it who need to tell their stories. Otherwise the Holocaust becomes an abstraction: statistics like "six million" and terms like "eugenics"—the pseudo-scientific basis for Nazi policies justifying their goal of improving the Aryan race by exterminating others—do not begin to capture the horrors that happened to individuals who lived through it. Watching, shortly after our arrival at Auschwitz, as my mother, sisters, and baby brother were taken to what I later discovered were the gas chambers. My father, in rapidly declining health, handing me his scrap of bread the morning he knew he would be deemed too weak to continue working and taken away to be killed. Can you imagine people doing these things to other people?

In the final months of the war, the Nazis did everything possible to destroy evidence of the concentration camps, of the scale of mass murder they had been involved in. Afterwards, it was often difficult for the world to believe anything this extreme could really have happened, but it did! As evidence mounted, the world has accepted that it did, but as time passes, the number of eyewitnesses dwindle. In a 2018 survey conducted by Schoen Consulting (now Schoen Cooperman Research) in the US, 31 percent of Americans, and 41 percent of Millennials, believe that two million or fewer Jews were killed in the Holocaust. The real number is approximately six million. Forty-one percent of Americans and 66 percent of Millennials do not know what Auschwitz was. Also, there remains a small but dangerous movement of Holocaust deniers determined to "prove" the facts are exaggerated or wrong.

In my own country, Canada, young adults show an alarming knowledge gap, according to research done by the Azrieli Foundation, an organization that promotes Holocaust education. Its results showed that many people do not know what the Holocaust was, cannot name a concentration camp, and are unaware that millions of Jews died during World War II. Fifty-four percent of Canadians polled said they were not aware that an estimated six million Jews were killed during the Holocaust. This is sad and unacceptable.

"Tell the world" is the emphatic command so many survivors heard. But for survivors, like me, after the Liberation I simply tried to move forward, rebuild my life, imagine a future that had so recently seemed I would never enjoy. I moved to Canada, sought an education, established myself in a profession, married, had children and then grandchildren. Things began to change for me. In 1994, I was interviewed by Steven Spielberg's Survivors of the Shoah Visual History Foundation (now known as the USC Shoah Foundation), which was established to commit to film first-person survivor testimonies. That was the first time I systematically told my whole story, and it was very difficult. After my eldest daughter, Audrey, went on the March of the Living, an education program to learn about the Holocaust, and visited Auschwitz, we engaged in many long conversations. Along with her sister, Alexandria, my daughters encouraged me to write my story, one small contribution to ensure the world never forgets.

These are my memories as best as I can remember them. It was seventy-six years ago, and the experience was confusing, terrifying, and traumatic. Sometimes I remember an impression; sometimes I remember what someone else told me or what I have read. Some photos trigger memories and they unfold still as I have been going through this journey to write my memoir. Historical facts, dates, and places are written about here as accurately as possible from my recollections, and any errors are inadvertent.

INTRODUCTION

Audrey: When I was born, in 1965, my parents lived in an apartment on Walmer Road in Toronto, Ontario. When I was four, my dad bought a house on Sonata Crescent in the Banbury–Don Mills neighbourhood, where he has lived ever since. It is surrounded by trees on a residential street with a big backyard that my dad loves. I would guess the first time I ever asked him a question about the Holocaust—not that I was aware of it at the time—was when I was little and pointed to the tattooed numbers on his arm. I remember him commenting once that the hair on his arms partially covered it up; I think a part of him liked that he didn't always notice it and have that constant reminder. It is possible that he didn't want to talk about it, but he never hesitated to give us brief answers to any questions we asked.

Alexandria: I don't remember how old I was when I became aware of the numbers, but at some point I noticed and asked him about it. He told me that's what they gave you when you went into the camp, so you would be referred to as a number instead of by name. He said they used these little needles with ink on them. He called it "my tattoo." He wore short sleeves; he didn't try to cover it up—although I never sensed he wanted to draw attention to it, either.

Audrey: I remember he told us he lived in a tiny village in a house with a mud floor and that his family was very poor. There were two families living in that house, his and his mother's brother's family. It was a type of farm and they had animals. I always remember him saying, with a smile, that he drank milk straight from the goats.

Alexandria: As long as I can remember, I knew my dad used to have a family. I knew the names of his parents and his siblings, where he was in the birth order of the family. This was the extended family I would never know.

Audrey: If my sister and I had an argument, just normal sibling issues, our father would get upset and go into his bedroom and close the door. He didn't understand how family members could argue. He would say, "You're so lucky to have each other." My dad didn't like to see any tension. It is amazing after all that my father has been through that he never speaks a negative word about anyone. Even if he felt that way, I don't think he would say it. And he is not a bitter person, which is also surprising and admirable given his traumatic experiences. He has always been a very positive and hopeful person.

Alexandria: I think my father would always be inclined to accept the human side of any situation. He likes to believe in the good in people. People around him might be saying negative things about someone—and I don't know if this is a coping mechanism that came from his experience—but he will believe there is good in everybody. He taught my sister and me to always do the right thing, regardless of what someone else may be doing.

Audrey: I am sure everything my dad went through has had an influence on the way he lives his life. He appreciates everything he has in his life, especially his family. I remember weekends in the backyard where my dad loved to soak up the sun. We grew up sitting outside or going to sit by a pool somewhere and taking holidays to Mexico where he had his guaranteed sunshine!

Alexandria: My dad wouldn't talk a lot about his experience during the war; it came in bits and pieces that I would try to collect and understand. I wanted to know more, but I was always worried about upsetting him.

Audrey: When we were growing up, whenever there was a movie or a news program that had to do with the Holocaust, my father would encourage my sister and me to watch it, but he always left the room. He wanted us to know about it, but he didn't want to talk about it. If we asked him a question, he would answer that specific question with a short answer and he would never elaborate. He later told us that he had blocked most of it out until his mid-sixties. I remember my mother saying that she felt my dad sometimes held things inside.

Alexandria: There wasn't much Holocaust education when I went to school, maybe a little as part of World War II history. I knew of one or two kids whose grandparents were survivors, but I didn't have a close friend whose parent was a survivor until I was about twenty and in university.

Audrey: I didn't know anyone growing up whose father was a survivor. I would talk about my dad and my friends would say, "Wow, *your dad*?" I came across the odd person whose grandparents were survivors but I used to think, I can't believe my own dad went through this!

Alexandria: He was always very loving toward us, but the first time I remember him becoming really emotional was when he dropped me off at the University of Western Ontario in London. He did not want me to go away to university, maybe because it felt like a separation in the family. I remember he was crying in the parking lot of my residence.

Audrey: Dad was over the moon when he had grand-children. When my first son, Blake, was born in February 1994, we had warned the staff that my dad would probably be very emotional. They cleared out the delivery room and my husband, Graham, brought him in before anyone else. He was so excited to have a grandchild and we named the baby Blake Alexander, because Alexander was my father's father's name. He was more emotional at that time than I had ever seen him. My dad always wanted a son, so having a grandson was a bonus. My second child was also a boy and we named him Cole Isaac after my dad's oldest brother, who was named Isaac. All of his grandchildren were named to honour his family, which means a lot to him.

Alexandria: It was really important for him to have a family here. He was overjoyed when he had grand-children. When my son Jared interviewed him for a school assignment in grade nine, he shared his story but avoided making it too upsetting. And he always liked to end off on a happy, hopeful note.

Audrey: My dad came when my daughter, Maddie, spoke at her school about going on the March of the Living and about how her grandfather was her hero. (Cole and Blake also used this term to describe their papa in school assignments—a sentiment we all share.) She asked him to stand up and the whole school gave him a standing ovation. He had tears in his eyes and later he was smiling. One little girl came up to him and said, "I just want to hug you." Others lined up to meet him and he was very touched by it all.

Alexandria: My son Harrison went to a performing arts high school. One of the shows they did was *Cabaret* and Harrison was in the key role of the master of ceremonies, played by Joel Grey in the movie. Both Harrison and I were worried about my dad coming, because of the theme of Nazism on the rise in Berlin and that at one point he would see his adored grandson wearing the striped pyjamas of a concentration camp prisoner. But my dad said, "No, I have to see Harrison's show." He said he had seen the movie, but he still had tears in his eyes as he sat beside me holding my hand. Afterwards, he said he was okay and that he was just happy to see how talented Harrison was. Later it led to them having some conversations about the war years.

Audrey: I think my sister and I started the conversation about going back to see Vojnatina, the village our father grew up in. We really wanted to see where he was born and raised as a child. I remember how excited we were to go on that trip and knew it would be so meaningful for us all.

Alexandria: My dad said he wanted it to be just the three of us. I remember Audrey had had her second child by then, and my first, Jared, was ten months old. The only reason I would leave my baby was for a trip like that one. I learned more about my father on that trip than I had ever known before.

PART ONE

1

VOJNATINA

ON A BALMY spring day in April 1944, a few days after I had turned fourteen years old, I remember the town crier's trumpet summoning people to the centre of our small village. That day, an announcement was read and we learned that all the Jewish people were to gather in a couple of weeks at the schoolhouse, at which time we would be taken away. We were given no more information than that. To be taken where exactly? We did not know.

Until that day, life in Vojnatina, our tiny village nestled in a valley in Czechoslovakia, which had been recently annexed as part of Hungary in 1939, in sight of the distant Carpathian Mountains, had been uneventful and generally peaceful. There were approximately twenty-five families in the village, six of them Jewish—numbering about forty Jewish people in total—and I had never sensed any anti-Semitism. I do recall someone once suggesting a Jewish family should move to Palestine, but that kind of sentiment was rarely expressed.

The village had a single, unpaved country road that turned to mud whenever it rained. Houses stood on either side of a river so small that it did not have a name, at least as far as I recall. The one-storey houses had straw roofs and mud floors. Our house was in the middle of the village—"downtown," I would jokingly call it today—and we shared it with my maternal uncle's family. They lived in the front and we lived in the back, so it was crowded.

There were, by 1944, seven children in our family: my older brothers Isaac and Artur, me, my younger sisters Friderika, Ludmila, and Irena, and the seventh, my baby brother Morris, who was only two. I was, at the time, named Simon; the switch to Thomas (Tom) came later. We slept in a bed like sardines in a tin, with our heads next to our siblings' feet. It was very primitive. There was an outhouse out back and we would go with pails to the village's only well to draw water. Our parents, Alexander and Rosalia, were warm and loving; they were farmers who had to work very hard, raising chickens and geese and growing potatoes, corn, and other vegetables as well as wheat, which they used to make bread. If one of us felt sick, we were given an apple. People kept apples in the basement where it was cooler, so they would last longer. My parents sold their products to towns and villages in the surrounding area and sometimes sold things out of our home, like produce, when it was available. In the winter, we did not have any vegetables or fruit because it was too cold for them to grow. Our family was mainly self-sufficient, eating food that came from our own land, although we were very poor. My mother or father sometimes had to go to another family who grew wheat and ask to "borrow" some flour. It felt to them like begging.

From Monday to Friday, we children went to a one-room schoolhouse where the teachers kept changing. One teacher, a man, taught us exercise, or what today is called physical education. Standing outside, he showed us how to dry ourselves after bathing: take the towel and put it over one shoulder and down the body, then the other shoulder and down that side of the body. I still do it that way today!

I do not remember having toys, but the children would play outside—I remember playing soccer—and there was a river nearby where we went to swim. Really, though, we spent a lot of time working in the garden, helping our parents. I loved climbing the trees to pick apples and cherries. Even now I love cherries and look forward to when they are in season.

When I think about my family, I remember that my father had black hair and a darker complexion while my mother was fair-skinned and had blonde hair, although she always wore a traditional sheitel that covered her natural hair. As a result, we children were a mix. My older brothers, Isaac and Artur, looked like my dad, as did my sister Friderika. Ludmila and Irena were fair-skinned and blonde. I was, too, with green eyes. Morris was only two years old, and I cannot remember who he looked like. Oh, how I wish I had even just one photo of my parents and siblings.

ON SATURDAYS, we would walk with my parents the two miles or so to Sobrance, a town that seemed like a big city to me. It had stores and even a movie theatre. We kids would occasionally go to see a black-and-white movie and watch the newsreels that ran first. I remember seeing images of the Germans taking over countries, but it all seemed remote from our insular world in Vojnatina. Our parents sold our goods in Sobrance. In addition to raising chickens, my mother force-fed our geese, opening their mouths and pouring in corn and letting them drink as much water as they wanted so they would fatten. After slaughtering them, my mother would sell the plump chickens and geese to customers, who valued them. You would cook the goose and also fry the fat, which was like bacon. It is called schmaltz in Jewish cooking. We put it on mashed potatoes or spread it on bread and it was delicious. My mother also took flour, added the schmaltz, and boiled it with onions. That was our soup and we loved it.

I remember drinking milk straight from our goats. We also had cows, which we would take out to pasture to graze and later milk them. We had butter, buttermilk, and a sour milk that was a little like yogurt. In season, we picked plums from our trees and our mother made lekvar, a wonderfully thick spread like jam that could be used in pastries or cookies. I remember going with my friend Albert "Al" Hershkovic, known as Hersh, a boy I knew from a neighbouring village, Tibava, to pick plums. What was a full wagon dwindled to half by the time we were finished sampling them! One day when we were cooking the plums over the fire, they splattered and burned my hand. I still have a faded scar, which actually brings a smile to my face when I notice it.

To grow our vegetables we needed fertilizer, which my father made by taking the waste from our outhouse and combining it with the waste from the cows. I also remember a rather sickening sight. When we looked at our own waste, it contained worms. They must have been inside our bodies. There were also lice in our tiny, crowded home. It is a wonder we survived. Of course, people did not live as long there. If you got sick, there was no nearby hospital nor modern medications. People often died if they got very sick. Although the village was peaceful, the living conditions were very primitive. As primitive as it was, though, that is all we knew and we were a happy family.

On Friday evenings we were all together for dinner. It was the only time we ate meat and white bread. During the week we always had a coarse, dark bread. We were a very religious family that observed the Sabbath (or Shabbat). It began at sunset on Friday and lasted until nightfall on Saturday. We lit candles and recited the blessings before dinner. Shabbat is the day that Jews refrain from the regular labours of everyday life. That meant not doing any work, creating a time of stillness in life. On Friday nights, a Gentile neighbour would come to our home to light our fire. Being religious meant we found a way to make our own "synagogue" since our village did not have one. The Jewish families got together at a neighbour's house every Saturday; it was a two-minute walk from our house, near the well where we got our water. We were not allowed to carry anything in our pockets on Shabbat, so I used to tie my hand-kerchief around my neck.

As for learning Hebrew, an older gentleman came to our village every week to someone's house where we all gathered. He travelled from village to village and was fed but did not get paid. He was obviously a very dedicated educator. Like most kids, I cannot say that I loved it at the time, but I am thankful for the lessons as I am able to read Hebrew to this day.

Of course, we had no electricity—the house was lit with oil lamps and candles—and, as far as I can remember, only one home in the village had some kind of makeshift radio. So, we were largely unaware of the momentous world events happening around us. We knew that in 1939, when I was nine, Germany had taken control of Czechoslovakia and parti-tioned it into three regions. To appease Hungary's rulers, who wanted back some of the territory lost after World War I, the eastern corner of the country, which included our village and was home to many Hungarian-speaking people, became part of Hungary. So, where we had spoken Yiddish at home and Slovak in the village, suddenly we were learning Hungarian and required to speak it.

Still, our parents thought we were blessed because we were under Hungarian rule. They used to say, "The Messiah has come." The rest of what was left of Czechoslovakia was aligned with Hitler. In Hungary's case, it had recovered from the Great Depression of the 1930s by increasing economic ties with fascist Italy and Nazi Germany. It joined the Axis powers in 1940, participating in the invasion of Yugoslavia and the Soviet Union. For the next three years, though, its leaders resisted the Nazi idea of a "settlement" of the Jewish question in Hungary. Our parents had been right: relatively speaking, Hungary seemed like a safe haven. But by 1944, when it was clear the Allied forces had won major victories and the end of the war seemed certain, Hungarian leaders quietly began negotiating with the Americans and British. In retaliation, the Nazis took over Hungary in March and changes rapidly took place. We Jews had to stitch a yellow star of David onto our outer clothing, and the Hungarian gendarmes, the police force that carried out most of the anti-Jewish policies, began supervising the mass deportation of Jews. I did not know all this at the time, but I was aware of the unsettling presence of the gendarmes, in their brown uniforms and caps sporting a rooster feather. Still, our family remained relatively sheltered in our tiny village in our remote corner of Hungary.

Until April 1944.

2

FROM
THE GHETTO
TO AUSCHWITZ

ABOUT THESE YEARS in general, I have memories that have grown in the decades that followed and even more so recently as I have focused on putting the pieces together. I have had the assistance of archival documentation and other information from various organizations to both trigger more memories and provide additional details. I know that between May 15 and July 9, approximately 440,000 Hungarian Jews were deported to concentration camps, most to Auschwitz, and before that to ghettos. On our appointed day, I believe it was in mid-April, we gathered in front of the schoolhouse where gendarmes supervised us. The six Jewish families loaded the belongings we were allowed to bring— fourteen days' worth of food and fifty kilograms of clothing—onto horse-drawn wagons and began the roughly two-hour trip to Ungvar, which is the Hungarian name for the city that had been, when it was part of Czechoslovakia, Uzhorod. We were certainly nervous. I do not think my parents knew what was happening, although surely they understood more about the potential danger than we children did but chose not to communicate it.

We arrived at Ungvar to find all of the Jews from that city and the surrounding area concentrated in a ghetto—on the site of a brick factory and lumberyard. I later learned a total of approximately 25,000 Jewish people spent time in that ghetto waiting to be shipped out. Officials took our names and we were given straw mattresses and blankets, which were inadequate, since the weather is cool in the spring in that part of Hungary. Perhaps we were in shock, but I cannot remember much about the three or four weeks we were there, other than seeing Hersh, my friend from Tibava, whose family was there as well. The conditions were crowded and miserable; we were fed so little we were hungry most of the time and the outhouses were unsanitary. I vividly remember one sight: our mother and father praying.

There was nothing to do so we spent a lot of time just walking around the ghetto. In Ungvar, the Carpathian Mountains were even closer. One of my brothers suggested we should run away to the mountains, but our father said no, that was too dangerous.

Had we known that we were caught up in the final phase of the Holocaust, we might have taken the risk. Incredible when you consider that Jews had lived in Hungary since the time of the Roman Empire before the Magyar, or Hungarian, tribes conquered the land in the ninth century.

Had we known about Auschwitz and the gas chambers, or that on April 23 Hungarian and Nazi officials signed papers stating that the destination for all the Jews was Auschwitz, that might have strengthened our resolve.

Had we known that during the few weeks we were interned in the Ungvar Ghetto the Hungarian government was meeting with the Nazis to coordinate schedules with the railway companies, arranging for hundreds of cattle cars to be available for the mass deportation, I think we would have felt desperate enough to try it.

Had we known the statistics, only available years later, that a Jew living in the Hungarian countryside in the spring of 1944 had a less than 10 percent chance of surviving the coming year, or that one of every three people murdered at Auschwitz was a Hungarian Jew, I am sure we would have tried to flee.

We did not know there was only one year left until the end of the war, so we might have been able to hide for that long. At the time, the calculation was different: we were pretty sure we stood a better than average chance of being killed trying to escape.

About two or three weeks later, it must have been around the third week of May, the Hungarian police began organizing us. It happened in stages and each family went together. Gendarmes supervised loading family after family into open cars—Were these cattle cars? I wondered. We are not cattle—with an empty pail as a toilet and a pail of drinking water. When about seventy-five or more people were crammed in, the doors were closed and bolted. We felt frightened and powerless. People were standing or crouching; there was no room to stretch out, which made sleep nearly impossible. Sometimes I lost track of my parents and siblings. There was no food and what little water we had was soon gone. The car was filled with the sounds of people crying, moaning, praying, dying. It was terrifying. At some point we must have reached Kosice, the Slovak city that had also become part of Hungary and renamed Kassa. It was the railway hub through which almost all trains passed en route to Auschwitz. On an average day, three or four passed through Kassa, each carrying 3,000 to 4,000 Jews, and by June the frequency was even greater. Our train stopped a few times so we could relieve ourselves and each time German soldiers would order us to turn over any valuables—gold, jewellery—to them. This horrible trip lasted approximately four days.

The train finally slowed and rumbled to its final stop. When the doors were opened, the contrast between the tomb-like interior of that railway car and the noise and confusion outside was overwhelming. Soldiers and officers in immaculate uniforms. Men in striped jackets and pants. Someone shouting, "*Raus schnell! Raus schnell!*" ("Get out fast!") Some details of what happened have been buried because of trauma, but I will never forget that terrifying day, and it was just the beginning of the ensuing nightmare that unfolded. We were in Poland, on the landing platform at Auschwitz. Much later, my daughter Audrey researched the records from Auschwitz: we arrived on May 24.

I was vaguely aware that there appeared to be large factories there, like an industrial site. There were large structures with smoke billowing out of them. The next thing I can remember is a German officer yelling, "You, to the left; you, to the right..."

My mother, holding baby Morris, along with my sisters were directed to the left. My father and I were told to go to the right by the wave of a stick. I had lost track of where my two older brothers were sent. It was all happening so fast that much of it remains a blur today. There was no time to speak to any of my family, not even to say goodbye to my mother. I had no idea where they were going, but at that time I assumed we would meet them later.

I vividly remember one moment, though, that has stuck with me throughout my life. My father, concerned about my welfare, said to an officer, "This boy is only fourteen and should be with his mother."

The officer looked at my father, shoved him back in line, and in German said, "Speak to me only when I speak to you."

These decades later, I have wondered if the officer was just putting a Jew in his place, or if he had judged that I looked fit enough to be put to work— there may have been a shortage of able-bodied men in the labour camp—or whether, perhaps, he looked at me, a nice-looking teenager, and saw in me his young brother or a son or a nephew and spared me. As hard as it may be to believe, there sometimes lay beneath the terrible authority of those uniforms rare shreds of humanity. I will never know the answer to this, but I am thankful for the decision.

I now know that if I had been sent with my mother, I would have gone directly into the gas chamber. My father and I had been judged fit to be put to work.

My father and I were moved ahead in a line to another area where we had to strip naked. This was incredibly humiliating. Our hair was shorn from our heads, underarms, and groins. From there we went through some showers which were either very hot or very cold. We were given blue-and-white-striped prison uniforms and found ourselves in another line. When I reached the front, I was asked my name, date and place of birth, height, weight, hair colour, and the languages I spoke. At that time, I was directed to hold out my left arm to a man holding a device that looked like a pen with a tiny needle on the end. After a few stinging pinpricks, I was no longer Simon Neumann. I had become A6837. It has faded but it is still there today, a permanent reminder for me of that traumatic period in my life. It is also a reminder for the rest of the world to never forget the ideology of hate that fueled Hitler's "Final Solution": the extermination of all Jews.

Our numbers were also printed on fabric and sewn onto our uniforms. An inverted yellow triangle identified me as Jewish but there were many other colours and more complex symbols to cover a wide range of prisoners. A red triangle signalled political prisoners, socialists, communists, anarchists, and others. A purple triangle denoted a pacifist religious group; the vast majority were Jehovah's Witnesses. A pink triangle mainly identified homosexual men, who were grouped with sexual offenders, like rapists or pedophiles.

A green triangle meant convicts and criminals, from whose ranks kapos were appointed. Kapos were the lynchpins in a system of "prisoner self-administration," which kept down the costs of staffing camps with Nazi military personnel. The Schutzstaffel, a paramilitary organization operating under the Nazi party known as the SS, assigned the kapos to ruthlessly keep order among the rest of the prisoner population. Many were chosen because of their affiliation with criminal gangs. They wore civilian clothing and had private rooms and better food. To maintain their privileges, they brutally oppressed their fellow prisoners.

The kapos could be even more frightening than the SS officers. They had been chosen for their violent, sadistic natures. Given authority, they were fearsome. I remember one day watching as a man was beaten and then the kapo urinated on him. Another time, after a prisoner had done something to anger the kapos, he was beaten to death. Our own people, prisoners like us, beating a fellow human being to death. The kapos became worse than animals. They would all be laughing as they beat people, enjoying the suffering.

It is awful to say, but under these conditions you somehow become immune to the violence in order to survive. I just watched, not that I could have done anything to save the victims. We all watched and knew that we would be killed if we tried to intervene. This is a time when you need to pretend that you are somewhere else. I found myself wondering, Where is God? Why does God allow this to happen?

During the first couple of weeks, I think I was in shock. I cannot remember much about it except the kapos yelling at us early in the morning, "*Aufstehen!*" ("Get up!") We would go straight outside, in all seasons, to get washed. Then we stood in a line to get a piece of bread and later some watery soup.

It was the beginning of my year in hell.

3

A YEAR
IN HELL

AUSCHWITZ, IT IS important to remember, was not a single facility. The largest of Nazi Germany's concentration camps was located near the industrial town of Oswiecim, in southern Poland, where many railway lines converged. The brick buildings had once been part of a Polish military camp built during World War I. It was really three camps: a prison camp, an extermination camp, and a slave labour camp. The prison camp, known as Auschwitz I, was opened first, in 1940, and was the smallest of the three, mainly housing political prisoners. A year later, a huge concentration and extermination camp, known as Auschwitz II or Birkenau, opened outside a nearby village. Among the most recognizable symbols of the Holocaust are the railroad tracks leading through the centre of the camp directly to the former munitions depot that had been converted into a crematorium.

In 1942, a slave labour camp, Auschwitz III or Buna-Monowitz—also referred to as Buna—opened outside the village of Monowice to supply the huge synthetic rubber and liquid fuels plant built by German chemical giant IG Farben with workers. Those who did not work in the plant itself were typically involved in construction or transportation. At its peak, in the summer of 1944, there were about 11,000 prisoners there, most of them Jewish. Aside from the brutality of the guards and kapos, the meagre food rations and rampant diseases meant many people soon became unfit for work. They were identified, taken away, and murdered. The average life expectancy for prisoners at Buna was three to four months. It made the cruel irony of the slogan, forged in iron and erected across the entrance to Auschwitz, even uglier: "*Arbeit macht frei*" ("Work makes one free").

About two weeks after we had arrived, my father and I were taken to Buna. I was separated from my father and placed with young boys in a barrack that may have been number 44. (I do not remember the barrack number myself but was told about this later.) The barracks were drafty wooden structures. We slept on three-level wooden bunks, all of us crammed closely together on each level. I remember my place being on a bottom bunk. Early every morning we were awakened by kapos shouting at us to move faster. We had about half an hour to use the washroom facilities and shower. The Nazis were adamant that we stayed relatively clean to prevent disease, even providing lice extermination services to control outbreaks. If someone was found to have lice, their clothes were taken and cleaned. The Nazis wanted to keep people clean to protect themselves from disease and to keep us working. There were usually three "meals" a day: a piece of bread with milk or tea in the morning; a watery soup, or often just tea, at midday; and sometimes a kind of potato stew with very little meat in it for dinner. There was little protein, and a constant, gnawing hunger was with me—was with all of us—every day.

Along with a number of other teenagers, I was sent to a *Maurerschule*, or brick mason's school, operated by a former criminal named Eddie who had become a kapo. The brick mason's school was where young prisoners who had not yet learned a trade were sent because the Auschwitz complex was expanding and bricklayers were desperately needed. We were taught the principles of building construction and then sent, as bricklayers or bricklayers' assistants, to build things like factories, barracks—some were brick, especially those occupied by Nazis—and air-raid shelters.

After the morning roll call, the routine was for work detachments to line up, with the prisoners going to the farthest destination at the front. One of the most macabre, although sometimes soothing, rituals was the camp orchestra. As it played, we were expected to march in time. Like most prisoners, I wore uncomfortable wooden clogs that constantly hurt my feet. After working, often at very hard labour, all morning, we were fed a watery vegetable soup at noon and then worked until nightfall. Guards would strike us—punishing blows with a whip or truncheon—for what they decided were infractions, real or imagined. If we were not fast enough, we were beaten. If we took too long a break, we were beaten. The detachments then returned to the camp in reverse order and the kapos reported on the numbers. The number of returning prisoners had to be the same as those that left in the morning. Even prisoners who had been injured, or died, were brought to the roll call. Everyone had to be accounted for, dead or alive. If it seemed someone was missing, the count would be repeated.

This was also when punishments were meted out for one infraction or another, like stealing food from the kitchen. Some were whipped; others, especially those who tried to escape, were hanged or shot while we were forced to stand at attention and watch. I remember being made to line up in the barracks and ordered to bend over so the guards could beat us with a rubber or wooden stick. This happened if anyone misbehaved or we were not productive enough. I remember one time in particular that I was hit extremely hard by something made of rubber. It was very painful, but I had to just take it and be quiet.

Finally, when eating our meagre meals, I had an opportunity to find my father so we could briefly talk. Having that connection was important. A man who had lived in a neighbouring village and knew our family told us one day that my oldest brother,

Isaac, who had been somewhere else in the camp complex, had gotten sick and died. We were both very sad to hear that. What about Artur? I wondered. Was he still somewhere in the Auschwitz compound? Was he still alive? What about my mother and sisters and baby brother?

To give you an idea of how traumatizing the experience of Buna-Monowitz was, decades later in Ottawa I met David Moskovic, a young man who was there at the same time as me and also attended the brick mason's school—and who remembers things that I do not. David says there was a loosely knit group of us, six or seven, who stuck together. He was positive that I had participated, with him and a couple of others, in distracting the kapo who was guarding the kitchen so another boy could run inside and steal some food. The late Israeli writer and Holocaust survivor Aharon Appelfeld wrote, "Child survivors cannot recollect the Holocaust the way adult survivors do." That may explain why some of us remember some things and not others. I have no memory of distracting the kapos or stealing food, or a lot more about my time there. Just fragments, although those are vivid.

One thing I do recall is our evening mealtime. We would line up with our bowl and spoon and one person would call out our numbers. Prisoners dispensed the food, which was a kind of thin stew that sometimes had some meat in it, from big kettles. I remember going to sit on my bunk to eat it and someone coming around to give me a little more on one or two occasions. I think sometimes people just lined up again and tried to get an extra portion, and on occasion fair-minded prisoners who were serving the food would select a few people to get the last of the stew if there was anything left. There was never enough to eat and we were all suffering from starvation.

At regular intervals, we would be told to undress to the waist and walk past a German officer who was examining our state of health. If you were thin and weak, you were sent away. We were not sure at first if these people were sent somewhere to recuperate, but we soon learned that they were sent to be killed since they were no longer useful. At the time, what we young people knew was to look alert, walk erect, try to hide any sores, and respond quickly to orders.

One day, my father, who had become more and more frail, was picked out by the German officer. Before he was taken away, he gave me his piece of bread from that morning and said goodbye. He had a look in his eye; I am sure that he knew. Had he saved that bread, suspecting what would happen to him during the inspection, so he could give it to me? This is a very clear memory that always evokes a lot of emotion when I think about it, and as I write it here.

You might wonder how I survived. I think it is because, despite the inhumane conditions, I somehow held on to hope. I would look through the barbed-wire fences—they were electrified and emitted a constant hum—at the Polish people walking by. I believe one way I survived was by looking at them and dreaming that one day that would be me, that would be all of us. One day we would be outside the fence, free. I held on to that hope, day after day, and never let go of it.

By the second half of 1944, the Allies were winning the war, although our only sense of that from within Auschwitz were the air raids on the IG Farben factories. They came on August 20, September 13, December 18, and December 26, causing enormous destruction. Knowing the Allied bombers were coming, the Nazis pumped smoke into the air—I remember it was so thick we could barely breathe—to try to obscure the targets the bombers were seeking. Later, we bricklayers were assigned the backbreaking task of cleaning up the debris, made even more difficult after the final two bombings because the cold Polish winter was upon us and the ground was frozen.

After the New Year of 1945, we often heard the boom of artillery in the distance. Planes flew overhead. There seemed to be chaos throughout the camp and we were no longer working. The whispered rumour was that the Russians and Americans were coming, that they would liberate Auschwitz. Freedom became a true glimmer of hope. But on January 17, that all changed when we awoke to loud announcements: *"Das Lager wird geräumt!"*

"The camp is being evacuated!"

4

THE
DEATH MARCH

MUCH OF WHAT I know about the coming days I learned long after the fact. As of January 18, Nazi Germany had all but lost the war. Russian troops were approaching from the east, their big guns becoming louder and louder. US and British forces had liberated Paris and were approaching from the west. Nazi officials, now eager to conceal their crimes, ordered all evidence destroyed.

To whatever degree Nazi control over the camps had seemed organized and brutally efficient during my time there, it was now confused and frantic. The three remaining gas chambers were blown up—the fourth had been destroyed during a brief prisoner revolt—although poorly, so enough of the shards of concrete and brick and gnarled metal remained for investigators to determine its previous use. The wooden barracks were burned, as were prisoners' records, although some remained. But how to explain the thousands of pounds of men's and women's clothing and shoes, the nearly eight tons of human hair? All of the luggage with families' names on them? What we did not know was that some of the SS guards, who wielded power over us like gods, had already fled like cowards to escape the imminent liberation.

As those of us who were able to conceal our starvation, weakness, or illnesses gathered, much like for a roll call, SS guards surrounded us with their attack dogs. It was a typical Polish winter, minus 20 degrees Celsius, snow and ice on the ground. Most of us had little more than the clothes on our backs. Some received blankets. Others managed to pilfer some extra clothing from the piles left behind at the camp. We were given a single loaf of bread, sometimes a little cheese, from the camp kitchen. Nowhere near enough food for the trial ahead. The sight must have been beyond belief: nearly 60,000 weak, emaciated prisoners trudging along roads and fields. The Nazis called it an *Evakuierung* ("evacuation"). Since 15,000 of us died along the way, it would more correctly become known as a Death March.

I do not have a clear sense of how long we marched, only that it seemed interminable. For the rest of my life, my toes have reacted very sensitively to cold weather and I have no doubt it is from the extreme frostbite I experienced marching in those wooden clogs. I now know our first destination was the town of Gliwice, fifty-five kilometres northwest of Auschwitz. Some locked arms and marched together to raise spirits and help carry everyone along. If anyone faltered, fell out of the line, or collapsed, they were shot. Being nearer to the front than the back was better because the effect of so many feet stomping through the snow left the footing treacherous. You did not want to be at the very end of this long procession because that was where stragglers ended up and were often shot. The same fate awaited anyone who tried to escape, although a few managed it. When a prisoner collapsed during the march, parts of his clothing were often removed to help others survive. Although it must seem incredible, at a certain point the popping sound of rifles or pistols was so frequent that I no longer noticed it. I believe we stopped at night in a town along the way to sleep in an abandoned factory. The cruelty of the Nazis had no limit.

I believe it took at least two days to reach Gliwice. There, at a railway depot, a long line of several dozen open-roof cattle cars awaited us with a foot of snow in each one. About one hundred of us were forced into each car. We were practically sitting on top of each other. Every few cars there was a special guard's car where SS soldiers kept watch, ready to shoot anyone who tried to escape. I was so exhausted and malnourished that at first standing or crouching in the railway car seemed preferable to marching, but once the train began moving, the wind made the cold that much worse. There was no food, water, or toilet facility. We had to relieve ourselves wherever we were sitting. When someone died, their body lay in a corner of the car. I cannot even put into words how horrifying this was, along with the wretched smell. I remember snow falling and I was so thirsty I would turn my face to the sky and let the flakes melt on my tongue. That snow was the only thing that passed my lips the whole journey. As we rumbled through Poland and toward the German border, several times we approached overpasses where people threw bread down into the open cars. I would like to think that this was a kind gesture, but there are descriptions of people doing this to watch the Jews kill each other for the scraps, such as in Elie Wiesel's book *Night*.

5

BUCHENWALD

THE DEATH MARCH may have been four or five days in total—I am not entirely sure—but what I do know is that it seemed like an unbearable eternity. The train finally arrived at a depot and we were taken out of the cars to begin another march. Our destination: Buchenwald, a concentration camp located on the north slope of Ettersberg Hill, in a beech forest not far from Weimar, Germany. I arrived on January 26 as part of a transport of 3,873 people, which dwindled to 3,815 as 58 people died along the way. I immediately saw that we were in for more of the same. Buchenwald had a tall, electrified, barbed-wire fence; watchtowers; armed sentries; and a gate sign inscribed with the words *Jedem das Seine* ("To each his own" or "to each what he deserves"). Like Auschwitz, I later learned, it was not one camp but a complex of subcamps, most of them located at neighbouring industrial operations. The conditions and brutality of the guards and the misery of the prisoners here were no different, perhaps even worse, than Auschwitz.

I was registered as a "political Hungarian Jew," given the new number 123418, and sent to the "Little Camp." I was at the time five-foot-two and weighed only eighty-eight pounds. On one of the forms the Nazis kept on all prisoners, mine read "freezing of both feet" and "additionally overall weakness of the body." Separated by a barbed-wire fence from the main camp, Little Camp had been set up as a quarantine area where prisoners stayed for a few weeks before being relocated to other areas of the camp. But with thousands of prisoners arriving from the Death March, it was massively overcrowded. Little Camp was made up of approximately twelve windowless wooden stables with dirt floors, each one designed to accommodate fifty horses; five military tents had been added outside. In the stables, we had to sleep on what amounted to narrow shelves made out of raw wood with barely enough room to turn over. There were between 1,000 and 2,000 of us in one barrack, which was forty metres long and ten metres wide.

At the end of January 1945, the Little Camp held approximately 20,000 people in the most squalid conditions imaginable. It was considerably worse than Auschwitz, as unimaginable as that sounds. There was no running water or heat; we shared one latrine. We were given only a portion of the rations provided to prisoners in the main camp. Lice was rampant and the guards did nothing about it. People were dying from dehydration, exhaustion, and an epidemic of diseases such as tuberculosis, typhus, dysentery, and pneumonia, not to mention beatings and executions. Some froze to death. Corpses piled up as the weeks passed.

Against all odds, I saw my friend Hersh—Al Hershkovic—there. We were both in bad shape by then and there was little opportunity to speak to each other because we were in different barracks, but I did think, Thank God Hersh has made it this far, too.

At first, I was sent to Barrack 57 and later moved to Barrack 59. I have memories of sleeping in a middle row of the four-tiered bunks, crammed in with other people without any space to move. I was part of a large influx of young people coming from many camps. Out of 86,000 prisoners, approximately 1,000 were under the age of twenty. Those, like me, who were between fourteen and eighteen, made up 85 percent of the children in the camp. There was a barrack created for the new influx of adolescents, known as Kinderblock 66, where Hersh and my cousin Alex were placed, but I was placed in barracks that mixed adults and young people.

On an average day, we were woken at dawn and scrambled to the washing area and latrine. The shower released a weak stream of cold water, making it impossible to properly clean ourselves. We knew we had only thirty minutes or so to make our beds, clean the barracks, and eat. Breakfast was a small piece of bread, some tea or boiled water with a grain-based coffee substitute, or a bowl of soup made from some combination of potato, turnips, and perhaps some barley or oats. Food was scarce.

I was sent to work in a lumberyard as part of detachment 20A, but, to my surprise, I was doing very little. I assumed at the time, that like conditions at Buna-Monowitz at the time of the Death March, things here were chaotic and appeared to be falling apart. Later I learned that resistance leaders in the blocks knew I was too weak to work but made sure I was on the work detail so I would receive my rations. Here, we were fed once a day, often just a weak turnip soup. People were dying daily from hunger, sickness, or brutal treatment at the hands of the guards. We spent our time trying to keep warm, huddled on a bunk and only leaving when we had to. I wasn't strong enough to walk and I recall not seeing anyone outside of my barrack. We talked about how we thought the Americans were coming and wondered how long that would take.

We slept on stiff boards without even thin mattresses or straw. In early March 1945, just over a month after we had arrived, I developed painful sores on my hip and tailbone. I grew weaker and feverish, could not sleep on either side or on my back, and could not walk properly. I think I developed bed sores or ulcers that had become infected or blood clots from lying on the hard boards. I cannot remember if I spoke to a guard or if someone else intervened, but I was taken to the makeshift infirmary, staffed by prisoners, in Block 61. It was mainly intended for invalids and it was known as the "Death Block": very sick prisoners were placed here and death was rampant. The "normal" amount of deaths per day was fifteen to twenty, but after an order in January to murder the sick by lethal injection, that number rose to fifty or sixty. I was fortunate; this murderous activity in the block was ordered stopped by SS headquarters as the numbers were said to be too high. This came into effect in early March, shortly before I arrived!

Today I look back with astonishment at everything that took place next. On March 26, I was anaesthetized, operated on, and stitched up. I now believe the doctors must have been prisoners, and probably Jews like myself, with medical training. I have also read that medical procedures like cutting out boils or ulcers were sometimes done to protect prisoners by keeping them in the relative safety of the infirmary for a longer time.

When I came out of the anaesthetic haze, I remember a doctor asked me, in a Slovak language, "Where do you think you are, Bratislava?"

I was confused. That is the capital of Slovakia. I was in such a feverish state that I do not remember whether I may have said things in Slovak, or whether they had asked me before the operation where I was from. I remember that there were other people lying on beds around me. Without proper medications, I remained very, very weak, and my recovery was slow; there were times when I vomited as I staggered down a hallway. I remained in the infirmary as April approached. I had no idea how near death I was; I can remember few details from this time. I survived this by chance, just as I did when that guard at Auschwitz left me in the line that led to forced labour rather than to the gas chamber.

On my fifteenth birthday, April 6, 1945, I heard over the camp's loudspeaker instructions for all Jews to report to *Appellplatz*, meaning roll call. There is going to be another evacuation, I thought, another Death March, executions? I wondered whether I would be included, but no one came to the infirmary. Later I learned that about 23,000 prisoners from the main camp were sent on another Death March to two other concentration camps, Dachau and Theresienstadt. One in four died, either collapsing en route or the victims of mass shootings. Some managed to escape. I also learned that the SS commandant had ordered the execution of all weak and sick prisoners but the proximity of advancing American troops prevented this from happening.

I had no idea, until years later, that there was an active resistance movement at Buchenwald. As frightened SS personnel ran away, members of the movement got hold of weapons and overpowered the small number of remaining SS guards. Although the official day of the Liberation is April 11, at 3:15 p.m., when American troops entered the camp—the time that remains fixed on the clock at the Buchenwald Memorial today—two days earlier resistance members announced that 21,000 prisoners were free. Lying in my infirmary bed, still feverish and weak, wondering if I was here to die, I was completely unaware of this historic moment.

The next thing I remember, American soldiers arrived and I was taken to the 120th Evacuation Hospital, one of the hospitals that had been created in former SS barracks, where I was treated by medics. These Army medics arrived to find a human catastrophe. Feeding us had to be handled with care; after long periods of malnutrition, many experienced stomach pains when they were fed, and initially some emaciated prisoners were allowed to eat too much and died. At the hospital, I was given blood transfusions, plasma, and medication and slowly, over time, fed a simple soup and oatmeal.

I have read many testimonies and watched interviews of American soldiers who worked in the camp for weeks after Liberation to help us in our medical recovery. The descriptions of us are chilling and obviously had a huge and agonizing effect on them as they encountered something they could never have prepared for. They described us as "skeletons with skin on them," with "skeletal faces with deep-set eyes," "heads shaved, ragged stripe-type pyjamas," "some naked with sores on their bodies." One soldier describes the hundreds and hundreds of dead bodies stacked up like wood waiting to be cremated and that he found it very difficult to believe that the citizens of Weimar did not know this was happening given its proximity and the stench that emanated for miles beyond the camp.

But the soldiers also described in us a willingness to live and that is accurate. As you can imagine, reading all of the descriptions and testimonies of what they found is very difficult for me. They were describing all of us survivors. They were describing me.

I later read a powerful speech by Elie Wiesel, who was also a prisoner there, about the reaction of the American liberators as they entered Buchenwald: "We were strangers to one another. We might as well have descended from different planets, and yet a link was created between us. A bond was established. We became not only comrades, not only brothers. We became each other's witnesses... You looked and looked. You could not move your gaze away from us. It was as though you sought to alter reality with your eyes. They reflected astonishment, bewilderment, endless pain, and anger. Yes, anger above all."

One unforgettable moment for me was seeing a procession of well-dressed German women and men being led through the camp, including the hospital where I lay. General George Patton, the US commander in France and Germany, had ordered 1,000 citizens from the nearby city of Weimar—mainly from the middle and upper classes who had influence in society—to see with their own eyes evidence of Nazi atrocities. Most were visibly upset; some were crying. Some women fainted and had to be helped away. I remember them staring at me. I was barely alive, but it is a very vivid memory. The idea, of course, was for the German people to take responsibility for Nazi crimes, not permitting them to believe it was all just exaggerated rumours. This needed to be seen.

It took several weeks but gradually I grew stronger and finally, on May 16, 1945, I was able to walk out of the hospital on my own. Decades later, my daughter Audrey made an incredible discovery when searching the Arolsen Archives, the world's largest repository of data about victims and survivors of the Holocaust. At Auschwitz, my brother Artur (prisoner number A7629) had been listed as a *Friseur*, a hair stylist or barber. I do not know if this means he was assigned to do that at Auschwitz, as I have no further detail than this. However, he survived Auschwitz, which I had always assumed was not the case. He was on the Death March to Buchenwald, too, but he must have been among the first to leave because he arrived four days before I did. He was prisoner number 11829; I was 123418. He was even in the Little Camp, in the same big, overcrowded Barrack 59 that I was in, although it appears not at the same time. I have been told by members of the Buchenwald Foundation that Artur arrived on January 22 and was not given a work detail but was in quarantine. He was in Barrack 51, which was directly behind Barrack 57 where I was (see Figure 4 in the Appendix, page 230). Then he was in 59 but it is not clear on which date. For four days we were so close to each other and never knew. It is too difficult to think about. On January 30, four days after I arrived, he was transferred to a sub-camp, Berga-Elster.

Berga-Elster had been around for a little more than a year. The plan there was to build eighteen interconnected tunnels in the Zikraer Berg mountain for an underground synthetic oil plant. Working in the tunnels was gruelling and dangerous; many prisoners died from work-related accidents. The large group of boys, aged thirteen to seventeen, worked in the kitchens, delivered food, and cleaned SS officers' rooms. Artur was nineteen. I hoped he had been able to falsify his age and escape the tunnels. The subcamp was closed on April 10. At that time, many prisoners were taken to Dachau, another concentration camp in southern Germany. Others were marched in a southeasterly direction toward Leitmeritz, a subcamp of the Flossenburg concentration camp and Theresienstadt (or, in Czech, Terezin), a hybrid ghetto–concentration camp where I would later learn one of my uncles had spent the war.

According to documents and communications we had with an archivist at the Arolsen Archives, Artur's fate was listed as "unknown." I can only assume he did not survive. I cannot describe how I felt learning that Artur and I came so close to reconnecting at Buchenwald, if only for a brief time. How I wish we had seen each other.

After I left Buchenwald mid-May 1945, the only thing on my mind was returning to my village and, I hoped, reuniting with my family. I prayed, needing to know if anyone had survived.

A replica of the cattle cars used to deport Jews and other targeted groups to concentration camps, labour camps, and extermination camps throughout Europe.

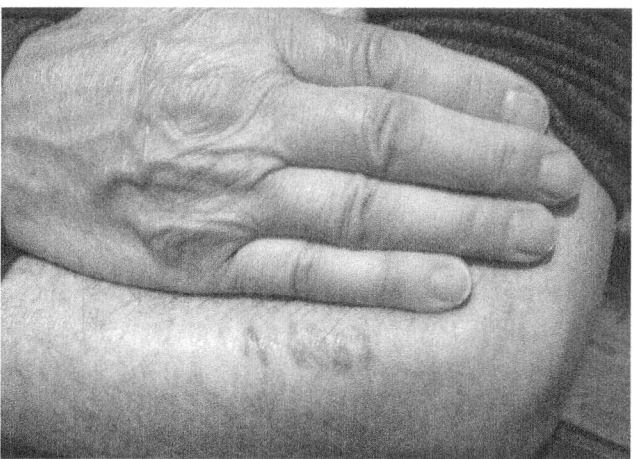

The identification number A6837 tattooed upon my arrival in Auschwitz is still visible today. See page 36.

Documentation of my arrival in Buchenwald on January 26, 1945, only a few days after my brother Artur (which I did not know until writing this book). My Auschwitz prisoner number was A6837. My Buchenwald prisoner number was 123418. Further documentation can be found in the Appendix. Courtesy of the Arolsen Archives.

Documentation of my brother Artur's arrival in Buchenwald on January 22, 1945. His Auschwitz prisoner number was A7629 and his Buchenwald prisoner number was 118289. See page 65. Further documentation can be found in the Appendix. Courtesy of the Arolsen Archives.

Patients in a hospital at the Buchenwald concentration camp near Weimar, Germany, after the camp was liberated by the Allies. This photo was taken on April 16, 1945. I was eventually transferred to another hospital. See page 63. Photo courtesy of the United States Army Signal Corps, Harry S. Truman Library & Museum.

Photograph of my Uncle Bobek, paternal grandmother, and young cousin in Zamutov. Taken in 1939.

Photograph of some of my paternal first cousins
who perished in the Holocaust. Taken in 1939.

After Liberation, my friend Albert "Hersh" Hershkovic (front row, left)
and I (front row, right) pose with fellow survivors during a stopover at the
Bratislava train station, en route to Vojnatina via Uzhorod, in mid-May 1945.
See page 70.

With a date during a fair in Budapest, 1946. See page 74.

With fellow students in front of the Institute of Modern Languages in Prague, 1946/47. See page 81.

Posing for a passport photo in Prague, wearing a Czech pin.

[LEFT] Walking with Uncle Artur (Bobek) and cousin Chuck in downtown Prague. See page 83.

[RIGHT] Holding cousin Chuck's hand while we walk.

During a ski trip in the Krkonose (Giant) Mountains with Bobek's nurse, cousin Chuck (hand over face), and his young friend. See page 83.

This photograph, taken in 1948, was used for the War Orphans Project, which helped young survivors of the war immigrate to Canada. See page 87. Photo courtesy of the United Jewish Relief Agencies and the Ontario Jewish Archives.

Posing with my first cousin Alex Ecker in March 1948, the day before I left Prague for Canada. Alex is a fellow Holocaust survivor.

[LEFT] On the ship *Aquitania* en route to Canada on March 20, 1948.

[RIGHT] With Johnny Freund (left) on the *Aquitania*.

[LEFT] Johnny Freund, Alex Schomberger, and me on the deck of the *Aquitania*, March 20, 1948.

[RIGHT] Playing shuffleboard on the *Aquitania* during one of the calmer days at sea. See page 94.

Upon arrival at Union Station, Toronto, 1948. I'm standing in the front row (with Johnny Freund behind), second from the left. See page 98. Courtesy of the Jewish Immigrant Aid Services Collection, Alex Dworkin Canadian Jewish Archives. © ADCJ Archives.

Sitting outside the Jewish Family and Child Service building in Toronto, April 15, 1948. The JF&CS supported us orphans with our settlement in Canada, including providing clothing, medical care, English lessons, and family placement.

Standing on the grounds of Bloor Collegiate. See page 102.

One of many dates during the early years in Canada. Photo taken at Bloor Collegiate in 1950. See page 102.

Wearing Air Cadets uniforms with Johnny Freund (right) in front of Bloor Collegiate.

Posing with my foster family—Celia (Chip) Forgang and children Suzanne and Bernie—at their home on 85 Rusholme Road in Toronto, 1948.

With my foster father Arthur Forgang.

In front of the Downyflake Doughnut Shop on Lake Shore Boulevard where I worked part-time in 1949. See page 103.

On a winter's day in Toronto, 1949.

Standing at College and Spadina with fellow survivors,
February 1949.

Working as a waiter at the Gateway Hotel in Muskoka,
Ontario, in the summer of 1950. See page 103.

My first car, a black 1939 Dodge.

With my first cousin Eva—Bobek and Gretka's daughter—during the Easter Parade in Toronto, 1954. See page 107.

6

IN SEARCH
OF HOME

ARMED WITH DOCUMENTS issued by the US military that allowed me to travel anywhere in Europe, I walked out of the gates of Buchenwald wearing civilian clothing I had been given. I could feel in my pocket my Provisional Identification Card for Civilian Internee of Buchenwald. Dated May 16, 1945, it was made out to Simon Neumann and bore my fingerprint and signature. I still had a number on the identification card, just as I had had a number in the camps, but this one, 5063, I guess we could call my "freedom number."

Where do you go after surviving a year of hell in two of Nazi Germany's infamous concentration camps, where you clung to the hope that this day would eventually come? I had nowhere else to go but home to Vojnatina. I felt sure my father had perished and I had been told that my brother Isaac had died, but I retained a faint hope that I might be reunited with my mother and other siblings. My memory of this time is very hazy, probably as a result of the trauma I had suffered. I remember at Buchenwald there had been some people from the Czechoslovakian government as well as Americans who helped me, arranging for documents that allowed me to travel freely by train.

As I was leaving, there was my friend Hersh. We were happy to see each other, and no doubt amazed that we had both survived. I do not know where any of us got the strength to make our way home, but I do know how thankful I was to be alive. Like much of this period, I cannot identify all the details of where I was or who I was with. The only stop I remember is Plzen, the Czech city famous for its pilsner beer. There, some people recognized we were survivors; some women cried when they saw us, knowing what we had been through.

There is a faded, sepia-toned photograph taken in this period after Liberation of eight people, two girls and six boys and a ninth person at the back partially obscured and wearing a helmet. Is he a soldier? Two of the boys appear to be wearing some kind of militia-like uniform. Were we all survivors from Buchenwald? Were the others locals who had greeted Hersh and me? I am in the lower right, smiling. Beside me is a smiling Hersh. We did not know what lay ahead but we were so happy to be free. I recognize that we are at a train station but Hersh remembered that we were on a one-hour stopover at the train station in Bratislava, en route to Uzhorod, which is fourteen kilometres from our villages. When I look at it today, I do not think I look as bad as you would imagine considering the struggle I had been through.

In this post-Liberation period, Europe was severely damaged. Infrastructure of all kinds—houses, apartment buildings, hospitals, schools, churches, shops, factories, roads, bridges, railway lines—had been damaged or demolished. Where bombs had exploded on roads or in fields, there were large craters. The war had also left behind a dislocated social structure. Many were suspicious of Germans of any kind. At one train station, there was a man wearing a leather jacket who some local citizens thought looked suspicious. They demanded that he show them his arm, because members of the SS had their blood group tattooed in black ink on the underside of the left arm, near the armpit. I do not know if the man had been part of the SS, or if he was just frightened, but he ran away and a few seconds later, someone shot him. It was important, I understood, not to be mistaken for a Nazi.

When I was close enough to my village, I walked the rest of the way, feeling very anxious, wondering whether my mother or any of my siblings would be there. There had been rumours in the camp that any young children who were sent in one direction with their mothers had gone straight from the train to the gas chamber. It was unfathomable to imagine that human beings could do this to other human beings. It was unfathomable to imagine this happening to my family.

Vojnatina looked more or less the same as it had a year earlier. Our house was boarded up, though; it looked uninhabitable. There were no cattle or chickens, and the garden was untended. I admit I was not entirely sad about the house itself. We had lived in such poverty there and I was ready to move on. Around this time, I saw my cousin Alex Ecker, who was a few years older than me. He had also survived the same camps as I had and was the sole survivor of his large family, although we did not talk about our experiences. Sometimes the mind erects a coping mechanism to help us bury the most horrific memories and I believe we were both trying to do just that. We stayed with neighbours who were very kind to us, but within a few days we realized that no members of our families would be returning. It was very different being in Vojnatina now, knowing that at fifteen I was alone, an orphan and a displaced person.

How did I feel? I think, after the time spent in Auschwitz and in Buchenwald, that I had become immune to horror. I had seen the extreme brutality inflicted on prisoners by the guards and the kapos. When the bombs fell during air raids, I had seen body parts landing right next to me. Without being conscious of it, my way of dealing with things was to block out the horror and resolve to enjoy life as much as possible.

I knew that two of my father's brothers lived in Budapest and one lived in Prague. I did not have their addresses, but it was a four-hour trip to Budapest and eight hours to Prague, so I decided to go to Budapest.

When I arrived at the Budapest train station, which was large with many lines converging, I found a city in ruins. I later learned that 80 percent of the buildings in the centre of the city had been damaged or destroyed and an estimated 38,000 civilians had died during the Red Army's battle to wrest the city from the Nazis. The famous Buda Castle had been gutted; an angel monument, built to celebrate the recapture of the castle from the Ottoman Turks 250 years earlier, was one of the few objects still standing in the city square.

I found my way to my uncle's home, do not ask me how. It was on a street that ran off Andrassy Ut, a major boulevard in Budapest. It had been a centre for cafés, restaurants, theatres, and retail shopping, with some beautiful mansions, although much of it was damaged now, and it also had the first underground subway system in Continental Europe. My uncle's name was Dezsö but he was called David, and his home was in a two-storey apartment block that surrounded a courtyard. His small apartment was on the main level.

When I knocked on the door, he greeted me and invited me in. David was a short man with a hunched back. He and his wife, Ilona, treated me well, gave me food, and told me I could stay. I slept on a cot in their bedroom that was placed in a tight horizontal space against the end of their bed. They were not well off, but this was a time when many people welcomed in those who had survived, and I was David's nephew. David and my other uncle who lived in Budapest, Simon, had been sent to perform forced labour but were not sent to concentration camps. However, David and Ilona had lost their daughter during the war so maybe I filled a void in their lives at this time as well.

I have a few happy memories from Budapest. I remember being on the streets when Russian soldiers were still there. I spoke a Slavic language, which meant I could roughly translate from Hungarian to Russian for them, helping them out. I also met some young people. One day I went to a fair with a girl I had met. There is a picture of us posing in one of those cut-out boards created for a photographer to take your picture and sell it to you. I am sitting behind her in the cockpit of a painted airplane bearing the words "Moscow, Budapest, Berlin." This picture gives so little sense of recent history—the camps, the authoritarian reign of the Nazis, the terrible destruction of Budapest as well as cities, towns, and villages all over Europe. In a way, it is a symbol of hope, of how life must go on and how I was trying to do just that.

David was a tailor and Simon ran a ladieswear shop. Part of my time was spent picking up clothing and delivering it for them on foot. David wanted me to apprentice under him, to learn to become a tailor. I worked at it for months, using an open-topped tailor's thimble. I think most people are probably familiar with the closed thimble that home sewers use. A true tailor's thimble is open at the top to allow for more dexterity handling the fabric when sewing for long periods of time. I learned to use it, but I cannot say I ever enjoyed the tailor's trade. I did not think it was the career for me.

David told me his other brother, Artur, a dental surgeon, had survived the camps and had returned to his home in Prague. I remember that Artur had sometimes sent money to help out my father and he may have visited our village when I was very young. David had his address so I wrote to him. Artur replied and made it clear I was welcome to stay with him.

So, one day I said my goodbyes and left by train. First to visit my village of Vojnatina one last time, just in case any of my family members had returned. There, I met my cousin Alex again, and he came with me to Prague. Later he returned to Vojnatina and eventually made his way to family (on his father's side) in New Jersey. We went where we could.

7

A NEW
BEGINNING

WHEN I ARRIVED in Prague I went straight to Artur's home at No. 3 Mikovcova, located behind the Narodni Muzeum. His wife, Marketa —we called her Gretka—greeted me warmly and introduced me to their five-year-old son, Charles, known as Chuck. Gretka took us to a nice restaurant where Artur, whom I came to know as Bobek, joined us. Bobek was my father's younger brother and he had been a successful and respected dental surgeon when the war began. He and Gretka, along with Chuck, survived three years in the Terezin camp, which was less than an hour northwest of Prague in what was then a German-occupied region of Czechoslovakia.

They were relatively fortunate, I learned. First, Terezin was a combination of concentration camp and ghetto, as opposed to being one of the death camps, and it served two main purposes: as a stopover for prisoners bound for the extermination camps and as what the Nazis described as a "spa town," a kind of retirement home for prominent, aging Jews whose disappearance might have attracted attention to the Final Solution. So, in that sense, it played a propaganda role to falsely claim that Jews were being treated well. They were not; conditions in Terezin were frequently grim and every prisoner knew they could be sent to one of the death camps at any time. They might not have received "better" treatment if my uncle had not been playing the important role of providing dental care to both prisoners and Germans; they were therefore protected. When he came home after the war, the Czech government returned his property and Artur was able to set up his practice again.

On the weekend Bobek and Gretka took me to their summer home outside the city, in Lesna, 140 kilometres west of Prague near the German border. When we returned to the city, I was given my own bedroom. Bobek owned the second floor of the building. On one side was their comfortable apartment and on the other was his medical office. There was an additional room on that side that became my bedroom, a luxury I could hardly believe. It was the first time I had ever had a room of my own.

I do not recall that we ever made a formal agreement about the living arrangements. Bobek and Gretka made me feel welcome and did not ask how long I expected to stay, and I had no intention of leaving unless asked. I loved them both. I admired Gretka who was a wonderfully warm and outgoing woman who had not known me at all before my sudden arrival, yet she treated me like her own son, as did Bobek. Best of all, Bobek was determined that I resume my education. He arranged for private tutors to come to the apartment, and with that help I was able to complete three years of high school in one year. We ate all our meals together and spoke Czech at home. But Bobek also sent me to the Institute of Modern Languages to learn English. There is a photograph of me with a group of fellow students. I am standing on the centre left, in pleated trousers, an open-neck white shirt, and sports jacket, looking very serious. I expect I was, as I tried to make up for lost time.

When I arrived in Prague I was Simon Neumann. My uncle announced one day, "I'm going to call you Tomáš," in honour of the first Czechoslovakian president, Tomáš Masaryk. I know my uncle really liked this name because he gave it to Chuck as his middle name. Now, I was Tomáš Neumann. I am not entirely sure if the name change was to symbolize a new start or if there were other reasons, but I was happy with the name and have retained it the rest of my life. Later I would make my full name Thomas Simon Newman.

One day while on the street, I ran into Hersh. We had separated, each going home to our respective villages, and he, too, had found there were no family members there and his home had been destroyed. He was living not far away, in housing provided by an American Jewish organization, as he awaited a visa so he could go to the US to his brother and sister who had moved there in 1938.

When I try to remember more details from this period, I often draw a blank, which apparently is not uncommon. The literature on children, memories, and traumatic experiences is extensive. Focusing on Holocaust research, many academics have pointed out that the experience was different depending on whether you were a child or a teenager. Emerging from the trauma of the Holocaust, younger children often had little influence over their lives after Liberation. They were in DP (displaced persons) camps until their future could be determined for them, or taken in by social service agencies, or sometimes simply found and adopted into families. Teenagers, like me, had more control over shaping their future lives. I recognized myself in passages from a chapter in a 2017 book by the cultural historian Joanna Beata Michlic, "What Does a Child Remember?" Child survivors "felt starved of knowledge, culture, and learning. Therefore, they immersed themselves in intellectual activities and pursuits trying to make up for the lost years. They not only studied intensely at schools, but also spent much of their free time studiously learning individually and in groups, so they could quickly be transferred to a class level more appropriate for their age."

Aside from my education, life with my uncle's family was like a dream. They took me to an impressive concert hall to see symphonies and opera, which I admit I did not really like at first—how many teenagers from a tiny village would?—but I came to love. Walking around the city, I could appreciate its historic buildings and stately bridges, not all of them damaged or destroyed. The historical Jewish Quarter in the oldest part of Prague was largely untouched, by bombs or vandals. There is a picture of me on a downtown street with my uncle and Chuck. We are both wearing double-breasted tan sports jackets. I look so young and I am beaming, obviously very happy to be there. In another picture, I am holding Chuck's hand, which I often did. In addition to their country place, my aunt and uncle took me skiing in the mountains. There is a picture of me with the nurse from my uncle's dental office, Chuck, and another small boy I assume was a friend of Chuck's on a ski trip to the Krkonose, or Giant, Mountains. I am wearing sunglasses and surely no one could imagine that a year and a half earlier, I had been liberated from a concentration camp. I looked like a normal teenager and my aunt and uncle always made sure I was dressed well.

We did not talk much about being Jewish and, in a way, I think I missed my religion. After surviving a Nazi camp, Bobek had decided he wanted to protect his children from future persecution. He belonged to a Czech church and presented himself as a non-Jew. Many like him assimilated, not wanting to be branded as Jewish after the war. It is understandable. Many of us, including me, wondered how, if there was a God, He had allowed the Holocaust to happen.

My aunt Gretka's friend Anna Weiss had also survived the Terezin camp and had returned to Prague
with her husband, Max, whose health had deterio-
rated so badly that he soon died. Her nephew, John
Freund, who was fifteen and had survived Auschwitz
and Buchenwald—I never encountered him at either
camp—came to live with her. One day, Anna visited
Gretka and brought John with her. He and I became
friends.

As time went by, political clouds began to form over
Czechoslovakia. A coalition government dominated
by Communists rejected the Marshall Plan, which
was the US-led economic recovery program to help
European nations rebuild. By early 1948 it became
increasingly clear that Czechoslovakia was going to
become a single-party state closely aligned with the
Soviet Union. Around this time, Johnny and I heard
that the Canadian Jewish Congress was bringing
Jewish orphans who were under eighteen to Canada
through a program called the War Orphans Project. I
was three months away from my eighteenth birthday.

Ever since Hitler had risen to power and the
Holocaust began, Canadian Jews had been deeply
disturbed. They began lobbying the federal government to change its restrictive immigration
policy that greatly limited the number of Jews who
could enter the country and help them get their
relatives out of Europe. Even after the war ended,
many countries around the world barred Jews from
entry. Between 1945 and 1948, refugee children

were admitted by very few countries; one of them was Canada. Although Canada had an unflattering history of anti-Semitism, in 1947, as a result of the persistence of the Canadian Jewish community, the federal government finally passed a bill allowing 1,000 Jewish orphan children to immigrate on the condition that the Jewish community assumed full responsibility for the orphans' support through the work of the Canadian Jewish Congress.

By early 1948, there were still many young people without families scattered throughout Europe waiting to officially enter any country that would have them. Jewish families in Canada expressed an interest in adopting children, although the preference was for girls and the younger the children the better. This overlooked a reality of the Holocaust. Only 1.1 percent of Jewish children who were alive at the beginning of the war had survived to the end. The youngest children mostly disappeared into the gas chambers with their mothers. In the end, 75 percent of the orphans accepted into Canada were teenage boys, many of them older teens. I learned later that this reality did not fit the profile being advertised in Canada in an effort to attract foster parents. The pictures were often of toddlers or very young children and one ad read: "There is a Jewish child, in a European DP camp, who is waiting for you to let him begin to live... he stands at your doorstep, needing a home, a family, the love and guidance of a father and mother."

The Canadian Jewish Congress had representatives in a number of European countries to interview prospective orphans. In addition to being under eighteen, in order to qualify a Jewish orphan had to be in "perfect health," express a desire to come to Canada, show proof of "orphan status"—that they had lost both parents, often a leap of faith since few had any official documentation—and "have the ability to adjust," however that could be proven in a short interview with a stranger. I learned later that caseworkers wrote up profiles that met administrative expectations that the orphans were "attractive," so they would appeal to the expectations of potential foster families. I realized years later that prospective adoptive parents in Canada wanted to be assured a young person was well behaved, serious, studious, and ready and able to learn a trade or enter one of the professions. Some of us were; others carried with them a host of psychological issues that might only emerge in time.

I had originally wanted to go to the US, because I knew I had an uncle in Pennsylvania. I had other uncles and aunts on my mother's side that had left long before the war, but I knew little about them and we had never met. The Canadian opportunity came up first and Canada was being described as a "land of milk and honey." It was also a young country, one where I thought I could make something of myself.

My uncle Bobek encouraged me because, he admitted, he planned to leave the country and come to Canada as well rather than live under Communism. It was clear that the environment of anti-Semitism had not disappeared. There had been some violent incidents in Czechoslovakia and Stalin had been referring to "rootless cosmopolitans," a thinly veiled term for Jews.

So, Johnny and I registered with the War Orphans Project. To obtain a health certificate, my uncle sent me to his friend, Dr. Paul Traub, who said there were a couple of spots on my lungs but they would disappear when I got to Canada and signed my health certificate. Again, I was lucky. Many whose certificate indicated health issues were not accepted. In my case, there were two complications. The paperwork had to be finalized before my eighteenth birthday on April 6, by now just a couple of months away, and my passport said I was Czechoslovakian (which I was, since Vojnatina had been part of Czechoslovakia when I was born, before it was absorbed into Hungary). The Czech government refused to allow any displaced people who were Czech citizens to leave the country, so the helpful War Orphan officials provided me with a passport that listed my birthplace as Krakow, Poland. I was instructed not to speak Czech at any time during my departure. In the confusion of post-war Europe, many things were possible that are impossible to imagine today.

On the "Personal History of Child" page of the paperwork, it read in part: "Simon gives us a very good impression. Although he looks younger than his age, he is personable and mature and intelligent above the average. His relations to friends and schoolmates are very good, his manners are friendly and direct. He lost his parents and 3 brothers and 3 sisters and he got to know the hell of Osvistchin [referring to Oswiecim, the Polish town where Auschwitz was built] and Buchenwald Concentration Camps. But he faces life bravely and is determined to get on and to make the best of the given situation." (I just read this about myself recently and, of course, found it interesting to see how I was perceived by others at that time.)

Arrangements were quickly finalized and our departure date to leave England aboard a ship was March 16. At various times I discussed the plans with Bobek and Gretka. It felt strange to be leaving them. I had been living happily at their home since the summer of 1946. They treated me like their own son, and I imagine Chuck thought of me as a big brother. Still, Gretka was pregnant and I wondered if, as much as I knew they would miss me, they were a little bit relieved. Their apartment would be filled by another child and I knew they were happy that I was going to a country where I would be free. They wanted me to take this opportunity while I could. Besides, Bobek promised to follow, and I thought we would be together again.

I looked up to my uncle. He was born, along with my father, in Zamutov, a small village in Czechoslovakia, but unlike my father, Bobek had left for Prague as a teenager, attended university, and became a dentist. Eventually he was named the head of the Dental Institute in Prague, taught other dentists, and became a surgeon. I told him that one day I intended to do something similar, to make a success of myself. My goal at that time was to also become a dentist.

Early one morning, Bobek, Gretka, and Chuck brought me to the train station to see me off. I had written a letter to Bobek thanking him and Gretka for everything they had done for me and reminding him how much I admired them. It was a bittersweet moment. I was emotional about leaving them but at the same time I was young and excited about this new adventure. I did not count but there were more than thirty of us, mostly boys along with some girls. Some survivors valued a group identity as a way of relating to others who had been through the same incomprehensibly horrifying experience. Others wanted nothing to do with being identified as a refugee. I fit more into that camp. I wanted to become Canadian and leave the past behind.

8

TO CANADA

THE TRAIN RUMBLED for about fifteen hours across Czechoslovakia and through Belgium to reach the seaport city of Bremerhaven, at the mouth of the River Weser in northern Germany. The city had been extensively bombed by the Allies, but critical areas were spared so the Allied forces would have a usable port to supply troops. After the war it was run by the US. We boarded a small ship and made the short voyage from the North Sea to the Strait of Dover in the English Channel. From Dover we took a train to London and stayed for a couple of days in makeshift accommodations in a warehouse in the poor East End.

One day, I went with Johnny and few of the others to see a bit of London. Near Trafalgar Square an old man approached us and asked if we were Jewish refugees who had survived the war. When he learned we were, he enthusiastically invited us to his home for dinner and to meet his wife and two children, a teenage girl and a boy who was around ten. I did not remember his name, but Johnny did: Phineas Goldenfeld.

When we arrived at the port city of Southampton, there awaiting us was a big ship with four giant smokestacks called the *Aquitania*. The *Aquitania* was an ocean liner, by then part of the White Star Line but originally one of the "grand trio" of the Cunard Line. Another member of the "grand trio" was the *Lusitania*, which had been famously sunk by a torpedo from a German U-boat during World War I. Throughout World War II, the *Aquitania* was a troop and hospital ship, and after Liberation it was transformed back into a passenger ship and carried war brides, migrants, and refugees to Canada. It was quite a shock the first time we saw the fancy dining room where we would have our meals. In actuality, the ship's decks leaked in bad weather and the bulkheads and smokestacks were badly corroded; we were on one of its final voyages before it was retired from service in 1949. But to me, at that time, it looked very impressive.

There is a picture of me and Johnny standing with our arms around each other on some kind of metal railing of the ship. We are both wearing suits with ties. There are other photos of me posing with one or more of my fellow War Orphans, and a couple of me playing shuffleboard. I do not know who took these photos or how I have them, but I am glad that I do. Unfortunately, what I mainly remember is that it was extremely rough in the North Atlantic in March, with huge waves thundering against the *Aquitania*, making it heave upwards and then crash down, over and over. I was seasick for much of the voyage, as many of us were. The representatives from the Canadian Jewish Congress gave us chocolate-covered cookies to settle our stomachs. I do not think I could eat one of those today.

Eventually the sea calmed and we were able to crawl out of our bunks and gather again. The kind people from the Canadian Jewish Congress told us about different cities in Canada so we could make up our minds about where we wanted to go. I knew I wanted to go to a large city but not Montreal, because even though I spoke several languages, French was not one of them. I remember noticing that Toronto, another major city, had a big and respected university and many other schools. I decided that was where I wanted to go.

I felt happy at this time, although I struggle, even today, to explain why. Part of it was the feeling of being free, going somewhere unknown that represented a new start. It was also that decision I had made after I left Buchenwald, resolving after all I had been through to try to enjoy the life I had been given and live it to the fullest. My friend Johnny Freund wrote his own memoir about his experience surviving the Holocaust and coming to Canada, and in it he recorded his impression of me at this time. He wrote: "Tomy N. [*sic*] was two months older than I. He was handsome, with a fine, chiselled nose and

chin. Tomy was popular and successful with girls . . .
He never suffered from self-doubt and depression, as
I did. At times I envied him." It is odd reading something written about you. I
would not have described myself exactly that way,
but I know that I was successful at staying optimistic, trying to maintain a positive outlook on life. And,
yes, it was true that I very much liked girls and they
liked me. It was interesting that on that voyage, to
the best of my memory at least, none of us talked
about what we had been through during the war.
Maybe others, like me, had blocked many memories.
Or perhaps we were all thinking only of the future. I
like to remember the phrase from Anne Frank's *The
Diary of a Young Girl*: "I don't think then of all the
misery, but of the beauty that still remains."

University of British Columbia professor emeri-
tus and psychiatrist Dr. Robert Krell, himself a child
survivor, wrote in a 1993 study, "The most pervasive
preoccupation of child survivors is the continuing
struggle with memory, whether this is too much of
it or too little." The latter is true in my case, but I
still felt compelled to tell my story, no matter how
fragmented, because people like me are the last survivors, the last bearers of memory. It is so important
that people, today and in the future, never forget the
tragedy of the Holocaust years.

ON MARCH 21, 1948, the *Aquitania* docked at Halifax's Pier 21, known as "Canada's front door" and

today it is the site of the Canadian Museum of Immigration. I had arrived in my new home.

A doctor from the federal health department came aboard to screen us and give medical clearance before we could leave the ship. Then we walked down a lightweight gangway that stretched from the deck of the ship to the interior of a wooden shed, which led to an assembly area. There were tables staffed by immigration officers who checked the authenticity of our documents, ticked our names off the passenger manifest, and gave us our official entry stamps.

There were trains taking refugees to various cities across Canada. A number of us travelled together and I remember looking out the window at the immense countryside rolling past and feeling excited about this new start. When my train arrived in Toronto and I disembarked, I found myself in a cavernous, impressive station—I learned later it was the Great Hall of Union Station—with a grey and pink marble floor and a tall clock tower in the middle of it. While Toronto was not as multicultural then as it would become a few decades later, Union Station was, in 1948, a cosmopolitan terminus. Almost all new immigrants arrived here after the long train journey from Halifax. Many of the workers at Union Station—the porters who worked on the trains, the redcaps who carried luggage for passengers from the trains to their hotels, the baggage room workers, and other employees—spoke languages from many countries and were sometimes asked to provide translation services. A few months after I had arrived, in a November 1948 article in the *Globe and Mail* newspaper, a reporter wrote that "the United Nations would do well to hold its next assembly in the lobby of Union Station."

In addition to several grown-ups from the Canadian Jewish Congress, we were greeted by ten or twelve young people, boys and girls who understood that we were Jewish survivors who had arrived from Europe. They were curious to meet us and friendly and, overall, the warmth of the greeting was almost overwhelming. There is a photo taken at that time of the group of us, about two dozen in all. Everyone looks excited to have arrived, and Johnny and I are in the front row, grinning from ear to ear.

We were taken to a large house on the corner of Harbord and Markham Streets, part of a downtown neighbourhood not far from a major shopping area along Bloor Street. It had been transformed into a reception centre for War Orphans and would later become an archive for the Canadian Jewish Congress. We all stayed there at first while the people from the Canadian Jewish Congress looked for homes for us. It was set up like a rooming house and there were volunteer cooks there to prepare our meals. Sometimes people from the Jewish community came to visit us and sometimes we were invited to dinners. Some of the War Orphans were adopted into foster families, while older boys like me tended to be placed in rooming houses.

I was at the reception centre for several weeks, sharing a room with other young men, before the Canadian Jewish Congress found us accommodations. Johnny Freund and I moved into a large house on Walmer Road near St. Clair Avenue. Mrs. Krauss, a Jewish widow from Czechoslovakia with a very pretty daughter, rented out rooms, and Johnny and I became roommates. The Congress paid the $15 per week for my room and board, and Mrs. Krauss made very nice meals for us. At the time Johnny and I sold subscriptions for a newspaper called the *Canadian Jewish Review*. A year-long subscription cost $2, and out of that we were given 50 cents. Sometimes I thought people did not really want the paper but they probably heard our accents, assumed we were survivors who had come to Toronto from Europe, and felt sorry for us. We saved our money and bought bicycles, paying them off at $2 per month. I was very proud of that bike, with its brown leather seat, white fenders, and drop handlebars wrapped in white tape. We were so poor in our village that I had never owned a bike and this was the first major purchase I had ever made with my own money. It felt like a real start at being self-sufficient and it was a good feeling.

While I was living at Mrs. Krauss's house, an incident happened that I am still ashamed of today. One day I found a $20 bill on the floor in the hallway. At the time, that was a lot of money. On an impulse, I took it and did not say anything even though I knew that it was wrong. Later, the person who dropped the bill was looking for it and I admitted I had taken it. That has stayed with me forever. I should have gone to Mrs. Krauss and tried to find out who had lost it. Looking back, though, I think that was a good lesson for me. It was not at all the way I normally conducted myself. I never did anything like that ever again. I felt uncomfortable staying in the house after that and a short time later I moved into a room in another home near Dundas Street West and Palmerston Boulevard.

IN THE LATE 1940s, Canada was still a young, provincial country and Toronto was a modest city, located on the northwestern shore of Lake Ontario, its boundaries covering an area about an eighth the size of the city today. Most of today's suburban areas were then still rural. It lacked the size and grandeur of New York or Chicago and the majesty and history of major European centres, which were gradually rebuilding after the war. Still, I remember having two strong impressions of Toronto. Compared to where I had come from, it was big, with large buildings and wide streets. And I remember writing to my uncle Bobek and telling him that there were so many cars. Maybe because everything was so spread out, it seemed to be a necessity for every family to own one. Bobek had a car, but not that many people did in Prague.

The population of Toronto at that time was around 650,000, of which only 50,000 were Jewish.

Most of Toronto's residents were of British background (73 percent) and religiously Protestant (72 percent). It was known as "Toronto the Good" for its dull, conservative, predominantly Anglo-Saxon culture until the explosion of immigrants after World War II, of which I was a part, began to radically change its character. Other changes were happening, too. Downtown, the main thoroughfare, Yonge Street, was torn up so a subway could be built and a new housing development, Regent Park, was planned to replace a neighbourhood of slums in east end Toronto. After the scarcity and hardship of the war, the city was newly prosperous, fuelled by consumer spending and a boom in house construction.

I moved around a bit during this time. At one point I was renting a room in a small house near Eglinton Avenue and Bathurst Street from a nice lady who needed the income after separating from her husband. When they reunited, I had to look for a new home. Next, I stayed with a kind widow named Mrs. Greener in her bungalow in the same neighbourhood. It is funny the things you remember. One summer night I was lying in bed reading with the window open beside me. Suddenly I had that uncomfortable feeling, a sense that someone was looking at me. Startled, I jumped up and could hear the sound of one or more people running across the stones on the driveway. It was probably just local kids but it scared me perhaps more than it would have someone else, given my past experiences.

Many of the newly arrived War Orphans went immediately to work, but I wanted to go to school and the fact that I had studied in Prague and was relatively advanced helped me. In September I began classes at Bloor Collegiate Institute and was able to go right into grade twelve. The teachers were very helpful. They would come in early to give me and other War Orphans extra help and stay after school as well. I remember they would say that we were a good example because we were so hard-working. We had to study a foreign language, so I chose German rather than French, since that was easier for me. I was still mastering English, so the only courses with which I had some problems were the ones in English literature. We newcomers were mixed in with all the other students born and raised in Toronto and I never remember having any problems with anti-Semitism. I did not hide my Jewish identity. If asked about my religion, I would say, "I am Jewish."

There is a picture of me leaning against a lamppost in front of Bloor Collegiate. I am dressed in a typical fashion for the time: a white shirt, a tie, a dark blazer, and grey slacks. That was the way I dressed for school every day. It was certainly not like today, where young people go to school in jeans and hoodies. There is another picture of me against a brick wall at Bloor Collegiate that tells another story. I was popular with girls, probably because they sensed how much I liked them and also because I had manners and treated women with respect. In this picture,

a girl is leaning in about to kiss me. I did quite a bit
of dating during these years.

One day in the spring of 1949, I heard about
part-time jobs available at the Downyflake Doughnut Shop on the north side of Lake Shore Boulevard,
across from the Sunnyside Beach Amusement Park.
I was hired as a busboy and dishwasher at 35 cents
an hour. I remember riding my bike there and enjoying the work. Downyflake was usually busy, the
people who ran it were nice to me, and I always had
a meal there during my break. On the red cover of
the menu was a poem called "The Optimist's Creed."
It read:

> *As you ramble on thru Life, Brother;*
> *Whatever be your Goal,*
> *Keep your eye upon the Doughnut,*
> *And not upon the Hole.*

In the centre of the restaurant was a black-topped
counter with stools; booths lined the windows on
three sides. I quickly got the knack of doing dishes
and bussing tables the way the owners liked it done.

The following year, in the spring of 1950, I com-
pleted grade thirteen, which Ontario had at that time,
and earned my high school diploma. I learned that
a resort in Muskoka called the Gateway Hotel was
hiring waiters and I was lucky enough to get a job
there that summer.

The Gateway had quite a history. In September 1939, Canada supported England by declaring

war on Germany. With Nazi bombing campaigns and fears of a possible invasion, the British worried that the invaders would free the German prisoners of war (POWs) they were holding in various camps. So, Canada agreed to house the POWs in secure internment camps. There were a couple dozen of these across Canada, and one location was the site of Muskoka's former Minnewaska Hotel, which opened in 1897 and closed in 1908. With the outbreak of tuberculosis in 1916, it was converted into the private Calydor Sanitorium for TB patients, which was finally shut down in 1935. In 1940, it was converted into Internment Camp 20, or Camp Calydor, its 500 or so German prisoners mainly drawn from the officer class. Some said it was more like a posh vacation spa than the kinds of camps that I, and others like me, had endured in Europe. After the war ended, it was closed on June 29, 1946. It was then renovated and reopened in 1949 as the Gateway Hotel, the largest Jewish resort in Ontario.

I had a wonderful time working at the Gateway. It was a popular spot, with many visitors from the US coming to stay. There is a photo of me standing on the grass wearing black pleated trousers, a white shirt with the sleeves rolled up, and a dark bow tie, carrying a tray laden with condiments. The Gateway was known for its cheese strudel and it would often run out before the end of the day, so I would put some of it aside to make sure I had enough for my customers. I remember serving a group of six young

women from the US who stayed a week and left me a
$25 tip. That would be about $275 today! By the end
of the summer I had saved $300 in tips. I knew this
work was not my future, but I had a wonderful time
there. I was young, spending my time off in a bathing
suit enjoying the sun and the lake.

I had wanted to become a dentist, like my uncle
Bobek, but I could not afford to go to dental school.
Instead, I decided to take accounting. I was not really
interested in it, but I thought I could earn a good
income and build a secure life for myself so I enrolled
in a five-year correspondence program at Queen's
University in Kingston. I remember writing what they
called a primary exam in my first year, an interme-
diate exam in my third year, and a final exam in my
fifth year. We also had to pass an exam in commercial law and one in economics before we could write
the finals. One needed a minimum of 60 percent to
pass, and only about half of the students succeeded.
During this time, I also started working three days a
week for a pair of small accounting firms that occupied the same offices—Stone, Smith and Conway,
and Smith, Winston and Wolman—to get the practi-
cal experience that the accounting program required.

About a year earlier, I had moved again, this
time to stay with a family who lived on Rusholme
Road, near Dundas Street West and Dovercourt
Road. Arthur Forgang and his wife, Celia, known as
Chip, became my new family. They treated me like
I was their own child. (It is very interesting to me

that three important people in my life shared the same given name: my brother, uncle, and my foster father.) Arthur was in the used car business—he had a lot downtown with a partner and also bought and sold cars from his home. Thanks to him, I was able to buy my first car, a black 1939 Dodge, which I loved to drive. Chip was a stay-at-home mom. They had two children: Bernie, who was ten, and little Suzanne, who was five. Later, Suzanne would say she liked me right away. I remember she put all her dolls on the sofa and made me sit down and then she sat on my knee. After that she followed me around everywhere. Sometimes I would pick her up and put her on my shoulder or take her for a walk. One time I took her along on a date with a girl I was seeing. We sat in a park with a picnic lunch and the girl gave Suzanne a charm bracelet. When I was taking the accounting courses and studying very hard every night, Suzanne would always want to come into my room, just to be with me. I would give her some receipts to add up, so she would have something to do and feel like she was helping me. She always called me her "foster brother."

Years later, Suzanne said she thought she must have been a real pest, but I never thought so. She was a sweet little girl and I always loved children. It is funny to look at the pictures I have of me with the Forgangs. Suzanne is always right beside me looking very happy. I remember Chip telling her children to look at me: I was well dressed, going to school, working hard. To the Forgangs, I was a role model. They made me feel loved and special.

During this time, Bobek and Gretka arrived from Czechoslovakia. I had once imagined we would all live together again; instead, I was comfortably settled with the Forgangs, and Bobek and Gretka were having a difficult time. Gretka worked as a cook at a summer camp. Bobek would have had to attend lectures and write an exam to qualify as a dentist in Toronto whereas he knew a dentist in Saskatoon, Saskatchewan, who assured him he could open an office there right away. So, they did what was best and moved to Saskatoon, although we kept in close contact.

I remember Gretka coming to visit in 1953 when her daughter, Eva, was five. It was Easter so I took Eva to University Avenue to see all the people walking in their fancy Easter hats and spring outfits. Then I treated her to her first corned beef on rye sandwich—she loved it—and bought her a spring outfit of her own: a new dress with tiny black-and-white checks and a red ribbon under the white collar. To this day, Eva says she remembers it "like it was yesterday."

I had a surprise around this time. Ruth Ecker, who was my mother's niece and my first cousin, and her husband, Jack Weiss, arrived in Toronto from New Jersey for a visit. I am still not sure how they found me, although they may have been talking to my cousin Alex, who lived there. Later, Ruth's brother, Morris Ecker, and his wife, Rose, also visited two or three times. I kept in touch with them, off and on, for years. Rose wrote letters to me, as did Ruth, and was very caring. Considering I had lost my own immediate family, it was quite an experience to connect with members of my extended family. It made me feel cared for and gave me a sense of belonging. Many years later, I would get to know more of the Ecker side of my family.

Later, around 1955, I moved with the Forgangs to a house on Deloraine Avenue in North Toronto. The living room was big enough for them to use it as a combination living room and dining room and take the dining room as their bedroom. There were three bedrooms upstairs and I was in the largest one, finishing my accounting studies.

It is amazing how Hersh kept reappearing in my life. We had been in the ghetto at Uzhorod, in Auschwitz, and in Buchenwald at the same time. We travelled back to our villages together and briefly met again as survivors in Prague before Hersh immigrated to the US, where he had family. It turns out he had a cousin and some friends in Toronto, so he often drove up from Cleveland to visit. We would always spend time together, driving around in his flashy 1950 Kaiser Virginian, white with a red roof. There is a picture of the two of us on a summer day somewhere along Lake Ontario, shirtless, standing in front of his car. (I recently sent this photo to him and we had fun reminiscing.)

At some point, he introduced me to sisters Erica and Vera Blum. Vera was a beautiful nineteen-year-old with black hair and a heart-shaped face. She was an artistic soul, a violinist who dreamed of a career performing with orchestras. We fell in love, and her parents, who had never had a son, treated me wonderfully. Her father, who called me "Sonny," owned Popular Butchers on Dundas Street West. In November 1956, the year I graduated and launched my career as an accountant, and the year I turned twenty-six, we were married. The Forgangs attended the wedding and it was like having parents there. Suzanne was a bridesmaid.

One summer Vera studied and performed at Tanglewood, a music school and festival in the Berkshire Hills of western Massachusetts. I remember sitting on the grass in the sunshine, listening to classical music drifting through the air. At moments like these, it seemed hard to believe that a little more than a decade earlier I had walked out of a Nazi concentration camp, one of the lucky ones who had survived.

PART TWO

9

BUILDING
A BUSINESS
AND A LIFE

WHILE CONTINUING TO work part-time at the accounting firms, I began to take on a few accounts of my own, working on them from home. In an unexpected twist of fate, many of my clients were Hungarians. In the fall of 1956, peaceful protests in Hungary for political reforms and independence from the Soviet Union resulted in a brutal crackdown, and Soviet troops and tanks flooded into the country. By the end of the year, 200,000 citizens, now refugees, had fled to Austria and Yugoslavia.

I reflected on how I had lived in post-war Budapest as a refugee with my uncle and now it was being invaded by the same nation that had freed it from the Nazis. I was also amazed to see how quickly Canada accepted Hungarian refugees without quotas. They mostly arrived the same way as I had, by ship to Pier 21 in Halifax and from there by train to various destinations across the country. Thousands arrived in Toronto, many of them young and educated with skills that allowed them to quickly find work and set up businesses. My advantage was that many of them, as well as others who had already established businesses here, were looking for an accountant who spoke Hungarian. My clients in those days tended to be small firms in areas like lumber, contracting, and plumbing that later grew into successful businesses and continued as my clients for years. I remember happily reuniting with Ruzena, who was a neighbour from my village of Vojnatina; we played together as children. She stayed there after the war for a period and then came to Toronto and got in touch with me. Along with her husband, Herman, she ran a catering business. We still do their son's taxes to this day.

Soon I was able to go out on my own, so I leased a small office on Adelaide Street West at Spadina Avenue, in the heart of the garment district.

I met a fellow accounting student, Gerry Shear, who was interested in working with me. We tossed a coin to decide on our firm's name; I won. So, in 1959, we became Newman and Shear. It sounded impressive, although at that time we sat across from each other at one long desk in a tiny office space on Adelaide at Spadina. One of our early clients was an emerging development company called Cadillac Development Corporation Ltd., a division of the firm that is now Cadillac Fairview Corporation Ltd., which was founded in 1953 to focus on building houses and rental apartment buildings. By 1960 it was growing fast, and the following year, Gerry, who had been doing most of the work with Cadillac and established a good rapport with our clients, was asked to join the company and he did.

Around the time Gerry left, I was doing some part-time work for an accounting firm run by William Walton and Harry Wagman. One day, I was approached by a student named Martin Sversky, who was finishing the same program I had graduated from by doing his placement at this firm. "If you need anybody to do some bookkeeping," he said, "I'd like to do it."

We needed a bookkeeper and I liked Marty's attitude, so I hired him. In a short time, he was handling a lot of clients and we discussed forming a partnership. In 1966, we became Newman and Sversky, still sitting at opposite sides of that long table in our tiny office.

An early client was a clothing firm located in our building. Joseph was an entrepreneur and his wife, Rosa, was a seamstress. Their best move was acquiring exclusive Canadian rights for Viyella, a British blend of cotton and wool that was ideal for bathrobes, housecoats, pyjamas, and other sleepwear. Their brand was a going concern in the 1950s and '60s; later, their daughter created an exclusive lingerie line that sold throughout North America.

During this period, another client was Magda Kemeny, who ran Kemeny Menswear on College Street. The Kemenys needed an accountant, so they called me and I began doing their bookkeeping. Magda was married to Bill Kemeny, a master upholsterer who arrived in Canada after the 1956 Hungarian Revolution. Bill met a fellow upholsterer named Saul Feldberg. Saul opened a small office furniture firm called Global Upholstery Company Ltd. in 1966, with Bill as his partner. Global grew from 3,500 square feet of rented space into the Global Group of Companies, an international giant that is still a client today, not to mention that Saul and his wife, Toby, are very close friends of mine. In fact, along with their children, I consider them family. Saul, who is a pathfinder and a visionary, is also a humanitarian concerned with everyone's well-being. My firm has grown in part thanks to its long association with Saul, just as everyone has prospered who has been fortunate enough to work with him.

As the firm grew, we eventually moved into a larger office space owned by our client Cadillac, in North Toronto at the intersection of Avenue Road and Wilson Avenue. We were successful, in part, because we followed the advice that we always gave our clients: we expanded slowly and we were fiscally responsible.

UNFORTUNATELY, THINGS were less successful in my personal life. Having lost my parents and siblings in the Holocaust, I dreamed of raising a family, but Vera was determined to lead the life of a musician and was not interested in having children. We separated in 1962 and agreed to a divorce two years later. It was an amicable parting of the ways, but in those days, you had to go to court and state a reason for a divorce. We decided to say that I had been seeing another woman and that was all the judge needed to hear. Afterwards we went back to Vera's parents' home and celebrated.

Around this time, I often played cards with some friends at the apartment of Henry Koren, a fellow accountant. He had met a part-time teller working at the TD Bank at College and Bay Streets whom he was interested in, so he invited her over one Friday night. She was a very pretty young woman, blonde with a round face and a lovely wide smile. She was understandably startled to discover it was not a party but just a few guys playing cards. When she said, "Oh, I can't stay," I impulsively jumped up and said I would give her a ride home since I was leaving anyway. That night, I asked her out on a date—sorry, Henry.

Jeanette was born in Scotland to Welsh parents. When her family moved to Canada, she first went to school in Winnipeg, then moved to Toronto to study music at the Royal Conservatory. She was a serious singer with a beautiful voice, but it wasn't her primary focus for the future. I wanted to take her somewhere special on our first date, so I chose La Scala, an upscale Italian restaurant. When the waiter asked her what she would like to drink, she asked for a glass of milk. I was thirty-two years old and running an accounting business; Jeanette was only twenty and did not even drink tea or coffee. She later said I had a bemused expression on my face. The next time we went out for dinner, she had a glass of wine.

Jeanette had a warm, generous personality that made her lovely to be around. She was the kind of person who could go for a walk in nature and simply be in the moment, enjoying every minute of it. She was a wonderful match for me at this time in my life.

We were soon engaged, and by then, Jeanette was working at a finance company. One night, a co-worker of hers, who was also engaged, suggested the four of us go out to dinner. We had a nice time, but the next morning her co-worker asked her why I had a tattoo on my forearm. After Jeanette told her, people in the office began asking her why she was marrying a Jew and making unkind remarks. It was very uncomfortable for her, and when she finally told me, I explained the history of anti-Semitism to her. It is one of the few times I can remember encountering this kind of prejudice in Toronto.

Jeanette's family was Anglican but not religious. In fact, she had attended a Catholic girls' school in Winnipeg and did not consider herself part of any religion. She often performed as a soloist at churches of various denominations. After some time, she began meeting with Rabbi Jordan Pearlson at Temple Sinai. She studied Hebrew, sang in Temple Sinai's choir, and converted to Judaism.

We were married on Saturday, September 26, 1964, at Temple Sinai. The reception was at the Park Plaza

Hotel with about forty people. Jeanette's mother, father, grandmother, and brother were all there. Gretka and Bobek could not make it but their son, Chuck, did. The Forgangs, my Toronto family, were there and Suzanne was a bridesmaid. Other close friends, many of them clients, also attended.

Poor Jeanette. She had heard that Vera was a wonderful cook, but Jeanette's mother had always told her to practise her piano and singing rather than learn how to cook. Once we were married, she tried to make her first special dinner for us. She set the table nicely, lit candles, had wine glasses out. She roasted a chicken, and when she saw that it was brown, she figured it was done and put it on our plates. When I sliced into it, it ran red and was still mainly raw inside. So, we laughed about that, opened a can of beans, and had that by candlelight. Of course, Jeanette later became a fine cook.

At first, we lived in an apartment on Lascelles Boulevard, where I had previously lived with Vera. Then we moved to a nicer apartment on Walmer Road. We were there when Audrey was born in 1965. She was an adorable, healthy baby and it is hard to find words for the immense joy and powerful emotions I felt. I remember once I was carrying Audrey as we stepped into the elevator; inside were some neighbours and I shamelessly showed off what I knew to be the most beautiful baby in the world. I loved it when they made a fuss over her. I had lost my parents and siblings during the war, barely survived myself, and now I was starting a family of my own. I felt so happy and fulfilled.

A few weeks after Audrey's arrival, for Jeanette's first Mother's Day, I presented her with a signed lithograph of Picasso's *Ronde au Soleil*, which she had always admired. It depicts children dancing around the sun. It was my gift to celebrate the start of our family and it hangs in Audrey's house today.

In 1969, the year my second beautiful child, Alexandria, was born, I bought a house on a residential street in North York. It was quiet, near good schools and a park. Jeanette would take the girls to the Art Gallery of Ontario, the Royal Ontario Museum, the theatre, the children's symphony. They took ballet, acrobatics, and rhythmic gymnastics lessons. Meanwhile, Jeanette was a paid soloist in churches, and sang in synagogue choirs and a Toronto Opera company; once, our very young girls had an onstage role when a group of children were needed. Sometimes she would sing out the girls' names, in her marvellous operatic voice, to call them to dinner. We had a neighbour across the street who would try to mimic her voice and it made us all laugh.

It was a nice neighbourhood and I became especially friendly with our neighbours across the street, Barry and Shirley Ross. What I most fondly remember about Barry, who was a little older than I was, is the way he would wait for me to come home from work so we could go for a walk. We did this almost every day. "Tommy," he would say, "it's good to be alive." Sadly, Barry died younger than he should have and he is dearly missed.

I may have worked gruelling hours, but I cherished every moment of family life. At night I often sang a Slovak lullaby, "Dobru Noc," to my young daughters. I always sang the first verse twice and didn't sing the second verse:

Dobrú noc, má milá, dobrú noc,
nech ti je Pánboh sám na pomoc.
Dobrú noc, dobre spi,
nech sa ti snívajú sladké sny.

Snívaj sa ti sníčok, ach snívaj,
ked' vstaneš, sníčoku vieru daj,
že t'a ja milujem,
srdečko svoje ti darujem.

Good night, my dear, good night,
May God himself watch over you.
Good night, sleep well,
May you dream sweet dreams!

Dream a little dream, oh dream it,
When you wake up, trust the dream,
That I love you,
That I'm going to give you my heart.

I still live in that house and love it as much today as I did when I moved in. If there was anywhere in the world that I loved to spend time when I was not at my office, it was in my backyard on a sunny day with my family around me.

I was at my office a lot in those days, though, especially in the months leading up to and just after tax time. I often had to spend weekends as well as weekdays there. The business was growing, and I made sure it was diversified, with many clients in many industries, in addition to individuals. That helped to protect us from the ups and downs of the economy. When Cadillac Fairview decided to take over the entire building at Wilson and Avenue, the company found us another office space at Wilson and Bathurst in the former headquarters of a construction company, which had gone bankrupt. At around the same time, in the early 1970s, one of our clients, a real estate agent, told us that two houses were for sale on Lawrence Avenue in North Toronto. We demolished them and built a three-storey commercial building, approximately 20,000 square feet in gross space, as an investment property with the idea of one day moving into it ourselves. In the meantime, an insurance company wanted to lease the entire building, which suited us. Finally, in 1985, we moved into the third floor and later expanded further.

I know I was not at home as much as my family would have liked, although I tried to ensure that we had time together. Sometimes I would take the family to visit the Forgangs, my wonderful Toronto family. We played a little tennis. On weekends we often went to the Inn on the Park, a luxury hotel not too far from our home. I had a membership so we could use the swimming pool and afterwards we would eat at the Harvest Room restaurant. For years, at Christmastime, I would take Jeanette and the girls to Acapulco or Ixtapa, a beautiful resort town on Mexico's Pacific coast about 270 kilometres northwest of Acapulco, where we would bask in the sun and there was plenty for the girls to do.

Another favourite spot was Masaryktown, a recreation centre with a pool and restaurant on sixty-four acres of rolling green space in the east end of the city created by Toronto's Czech and Slovak community. It was named after Tomáš Masaryk, the founder of the first independent and democratic Czechoslovakia and, you may remember, the Czech hero after whom my uncle in Prague named me.

Sometimes we visited my aunt and uncle, Gretka and Bobek, in Saskatoon, but more often they came to Toronto, where I would put them up in the beautiful Windsor Arms Hotel. Bobek was often working, so Gretka, who had friends in Toronto, came more often. Among Gretka's friends were Hedy and Francis Stevens. We became good friends with them as well. Hedy was an art consultant and Francis, a businessman and artist; I have some of his canvases hanging in my home and office. We also saw Gretka and Bobek's friends Maru and Paul Traub. Paul was my uncle's friend, the doctor in Prague who, despite detecting some spots on my lungs, had given me a clean bill of health so I would be accepted into the War Orphans Project.

One year I took the family on a six-week vacation to southern Switzerland to stay at the Aminona, a resort in a village on the right bank of the Rhone River. Maru's son, Andy, was the manager of the resort and lived there with his wife, Veronica. They were wonderful hosts. Veronica and Jeanette really hit it off, and the girls made friends with children from various countries. Another year we went to Wales, where Jeanette's family was from, as well as Holland, Yugoslavia, and Italy. The children teased me when I was nervous about getting on a ferry to the island of Capri. I had memories of being seasick for much of the trip to Canada on the *Aquitania*, but the girls were young then and didn't know about that.

I remember once when Alexandria was maybe ten or eleven and knew that Bobek and Gretka were also survivors, she asked Gretka a question about her religion. I tried to steer the conversation elsewhere, because I did not want her to upset Gretka. But Gretka said, "No, no, it's okay." She explained that they did not have any religion because of what had happened in Europe. "You can't imagine what it was like," she said. "Being Jewish, where we lived, caused a lot of pain for our family." She told Alexandria that children in school called her a pig because she was Jewish and that there was persecution during the war; she never wanted her children to have to experience that. Gretka was much more direct and forthright than I was when talking about these difficult times.

10

STEVEN SPIELBERG'S SURVIVORS OF THE SHOAH

A TURNING POINT FOR me in confronting my memories of the past came many years later, in 1994, the year after Steven Spielberg's powerful movie *Schindler's List* was released. The director created a non-profit organization called Survivors of the Shoah Visual History Foundation, today called the USC Shoah Foundation. The ambitious goal was to film the testimony of as many survivors as possible. In addition to the headquarters in Los Angeles, offices opened in New York and Toronto, and there was quite a bit of publicity about it. My daughters heard about this initiative, and Alexandria reached out to the foundation to tell them about me. On December 1, 1994, a nice young woman named Janice came to my home with a cameraman to interview me. Audrey and Alexandria were there, but they had been instructed not to be present during the interview. I admit I was nervous. I put on a white shirt and a simple red-patterned tie, which I thought seemed right for the occasion. It was the first time I had ever talked at length about my experience during the war.

I did not think it had affected my day-to-day life very much. When my daughters asked me about the past, I would answer their questions but not go into a lot of detail. I do not know if I had blocked it out or just chose not to think about it. I had been thinking about the past more as I grew older.

When I learned that the German government was offering compensation in the form of pensions and social welfare payments to survivors, I applied. I had to see a psychiatrist who said I seemed pretty well adjusted. The German government had decided that anyone who survived the Holocaust had to be affected in some way, and I was paid a small lump sum to recognize my unpaid labour while working at the IG Farben plant at Auschwitz, as well as a monthly pension. I applied even though no amount of money could compensate anyone for what happened.

As I took the interviewer through my childhood, my family being rounded up with the other Jewish families in our village, the train to Auschwitz, and the confusion there when we were separated, I felt powerful feelings welling up inside. I cannot watch my interview; it still makes me uncomfortable. I remember being on the verge of tears as I described the moment when my father was taken away and he gave me his piece of bread. Later, as I told the interviewer, Janice, about Buchenwald, I explained, "They would call the Jewish people together and we found out they took them to the woods—Buchen*wald* means woods—and they were shooting them because the Americans were getting closer. This again saved me because I was in this hospital and they did not bother us. Otherwise I probably would have been taken into the nearby woods and shot also."

At the end, Janice asked me, "If you had one message that you want to tell the world about your experience in the camps, living in the Holocaust, what would you say?" I said, "I would like to say that this will never happen again to any people. And I am confident that it will not. The world is much smaller now, people know what goes on, and I do not think that the nations would again stand idle and do nothing after what happened... I do not think this will happen again. We will not let it happen."

11

REBUILDING
A LIFE

B Y THE LATE 1970s, my marriage with Jeanette was increasingly strained. When you spend that much time at work, your personal life is liable to suffer. We separated in 1980, with Audrey, who was then fifteen, electing to stay in the house with me to continue at her high school. I was feeling very low through this period, especially when I was at home, and Audrey was wonderfully attentive, spending a lot of time with me. Alexandria, who was only eleven, went with her mother but I still saw her regularly. Three years later, Jeanette and I decided to try again to make it work. We even saw a counsellor. Perhaps it was too late. We finally divorced in 1988. There are many reasons these things happen, and despite our differences, I loved Jeanette and she was a most wonderful mother to our children. We have maintained friendly relations ever since, celebrating special occasions together with our children and grandchildren.

Looking back, it must surely relate to my past that it became so important for me to have the family together. I was not keen on the idea that Audrey study French at a summer camp in France because she would be on her own so far away. We never sent our girls to overnight camp with their friends until they were older because we enjoyed our summer trips together. When it came time for Audrey to go to university, she had just met Graham and decided to stay in Toronto for her undergraduate studies and law school, but Alexandria ventured farther. I was unhappy when she decided to study psychology and social work at the University of Western Ontario in London, about a two-hour drive away. When I dropped her off at her residence, I felt very emotional because she would be separated from me. Having lost my family in childhood has made me want to keep my family close.

Eventually, both my daughters married and started families of their own. I had known Audrey's husband, Graham, since they began dating in Audrey's final year of high school. I became very good friends with Graham's parents, Valerie and Eddie. Audrey and Graham had two sons—Blake, who was born in 1994, and Cole, born two years later—followed by a daughter, Madison, born in 1999. Unfortunately, like my own marriages, Alexandria's ended in divorce but she gave me two wonderful grandsons, Jared, born in 1996, just six weeks after Cole, and Harrison in 2001. Happily,

Alexandria remains on friendly terms with her former husband, Brad.

Over the coming years, I dated a little but never met anyone who seemed right for me. How ironic that she was right under my nose all that time. Grace Lindover had grown up in Toronto's Jewish neighbourhood near Kensington Market, her father a barber and her mother a homemaker. By 1976, she had been married and divorced; at forty and raising two boys, she came to work at Newman and Sversky as a receptionist and typist. She quickly proved herself indispensable, becoming more of an office manager, ordering supplies and proofreading everything before it left the office. I found I could talk easily to her, and within the workplace environment, we became friends, sometimes going out for lunch or coffee when we were both working long hours around tax time.

A few years after my divorce, I asked Grace out on a date and soon we were a couple. For years we maintained our separate homes until, finally, in 2004, Grace sold her house and moved in with me.

12

A RETURN TO VOJNATINA

FOR YEARS, AUDREY, Alexandria, and I had talked about visiting my home village of Vojnatina, and in 1997 we decided to do it. I had already made one trip there a few years earlier with my friend and fellow survivor Harry Ralston, who was in the lumber business and was also a client. Harry and his wife, Rita, Grace, and I flew to Prague and hired a driver to take us to Harry's village of Nitra, near Bratislava, and then to Vojnatina. But when Audrey and Alexandria and I had talked about it, I realized how much it would mean to me to show my daughters where I was from. It would be a bonding experience.

So, in the summer, when Audrey's second child, Cole, and Alexandria's first, Jared, were both about one year old, we decided the time had come. When we arrived in Prague, memories came flooding back. It was the city where I had lived with Bobek, Gretka, and young Chuck, where I felt like life had started over again for me. After settling into the

Hotel Hoffmeister in the centre of the city, I showed them No. 3 Mikovcova, where I had lived with the family, and some of the local sights, like the Narodni Muzeum and the medieval Charles Bridge that spans the Vltava River, with its statue of Jesus on the cross accompanied by Hebrew writing that reads, "Holy, Holy, Holy is the Lord of Hosts." That is a complicated story, but the short version is that in the seventeenth century a local Jew was charged with blasphemy and ordered to pay for the Hebrew text to be inscribed. When we reached Wenceslas Square, the centre of business, political, and cultural life in Prague, I was amazed that it looked much the way I remembered it from the late 1940s.

For some reason, when I lived in Prague with my aunt and uncle, I never went to the Jewish Quarter (Josefov). When I took Audrey and Alexandria there, it filled us with awe. Jews have lived in Prague since the tenth century, and at the Old Jewish Cemetery there are at least 100,000 bodies buried beneath the dense forest of tombstones, many of them tilted at odd angles. We also visited the Pinkas Synagogue, which is a memorial to those who died in the Holocaust.

When we were not walking around the city, we spent a lot of time sitting in cafés. I remember talking about the past more than I ever had before. I told them about studying English at the Institute of Modern Languages and going with my aunt and uncle to the theatre and to the symphony. My time

living in Prague, as a young survivor, was spent looking into the future rather than the past.

From Prague we flew to Kosice, the largest city
in eastern Slovakia, where I had booked us rooms
in a lovely hotel surrounded by forest a couple of
miles outside the city. The next day, our hired driver,
Vlada, took us to Vojnatina. (It was not expensive and
seemed easier than driving ourselves.) My daughters were fascinated by Vojnatina; there is a picture
of them standing beside the town sign looking as
though they can hardly believe they are visiting
the place I had told them about for so many years.
Despite the beautiful countryside, though, it is a
rather sad little village, not prosperous at all. It looks
like most people, especially the younger ones, have
moved to larger towns or cities.

There is a general store that sits where my
childhood home once stood. A few men were sitting on the steps, staring at us. We were dressed
in casual North American sportswear—shorts and
jerseys—so I guess no one would mistake us for
locals. Later, the girls said, "We stuck out like a sore
thumb." I showed my daughters the land beside and
behind the general store, which had once been our
garden and outhouse. When I went into the store and
spoke to the proprietor, he was not very friendly.

Word spreads quickly in a tiny place like Vojnatina
and soon we encountered Maria, who had remembered me from my previous visit. Maria used to play
with my eldest sister, Friderika, and with me as well.

The village was so small, all the children played together. As we chatted, she began to cry. I had to later translate for Audrey and Alexandria that Maria was saying that she was so sorry, she did not know what they were doing back in 1944. I comforted her, telling her she was just a child, she could not have known or done anything even if she had known.

Maria became our tour guide. She explained that the store owner may have been nervous because I had once owned the property and might want it back. (Many years ago, I had hired someone to look into whether I could reclaim my family's property but decided it was not worth pursuing.) We walked around the village with Maria until she brought us to her backyard where she served us lunch that included some homemade jams. Another lady, whose name I have now forgotten, with grey hair and a flowered dress, joined us. She remembered my parents and told me that I most resembled my mother. One of the girls took a lovely picture of Maria and me staring up at her impressive apricot tree. Later, as we continued our stroll through the village, we met a nice lady wearing a red print dress who told me that she was the neighbour who used to light my parents' fire on Shabbat.

Finally, as we were preparing to leave, I hugged Maria. She had been so hospitable and happy to see me. She had tears in her eyes and so did I. As I told Audrey and Alexandria later, I knew I would not be returning to Vojnatina, so I would never be seeing

Maria again. I felt sad to think about this being the last time I would see my childhood home.

I was feeling rather melancholy as we made the hour-long drive to Zamutov, my father's hometown. At one point we stopped at a World War II memorial with a tank and other monuments, an odd reminder of my childhood. The girls took a picture standing outside a boarded-up, one-storey building where my grandfather lived and operated a small store. I was young, but I can remember going to Zamutov to visit our relatives and being sick on the bus ride there. Then I ran into a man, older than I was, wearing a brown sweater and pants and a battered brown hat. He told me he remembered my grandfather's store and talked a bit about my family, which was really nice for me.

A couple of days later, we flew from Prague back to Toronto. I find it difficult to explain how I felt. A warmth that I could have such a wonderful trip with my daughters and show them where I am from. And at the same time, a satisfaction and pride that I had survived and built a successful career and family in Toronto, where I live in comfort that was unimaginable to me as a child.

Reminiscing recently with Hersh about days spent driving around in his 1950 Kaiser Virginian.

At Lake Ontario with Hersh, early 1950s. See page 108.

With my first wife, Vera Blum. See page 108.

Alex Schomberger and me, tennis champions, May 1952.

Wedding day with Jeanette, September 26, 1964.
See page 120.

With Morris Ecker (my maternal first cousin) during his trip to Toronto,
circa 1970s.

Posing at a photo shoot with Audrey.

Having fun at home with Alexandria.

Audrey and Alexandria, a father's pride and joy.

Visiting with Bobek and Gretka at their home in Saskatoon, Saskatchewan, in August 1973. They left Czechoslovakia in 1949.

Holding my first grandchild, Blake, during his bris in February 1994.

Meeting Pope John Paul II in April 1994 after the Papal Concert to Commemorate the Shoah, the first official recognition by the Vatican of the atrocities committed against the Jewish people during the Holocaust. See page 150.

An emotional moment in 1997, seeing my daughters at my village sign when I took them to see where I was from. See page 14.

A general store now sits where my childhood home once stood. The land adjacent to and behind the general store had been the garden and the outhouse.

Looking at an apricot tree with Maria, a local who grew up in Vojnatina with me and my siblings. See page 144.

After walking through the village with Maria, she generously served us a delicious lunch in her backyard.

On the fifty-first anniversary of the end of the Second World War on
May 13, 1996, I was recognized as a Holocaust survivor and presented with
a document by Premier of Ontario Michael D. Harris. See pages 150 and 236.

September 28, 2000

THE CANADIAN JEWISH NEWS

Greater Toronto Area

A time to remember..

September 28 / 2000

TWO GENERATIONS REMEMBER: Holocaust survivor Thomas Newman
and his grandson Blake Rosenberg, 6, light one of the six commemorative candles at the
Canadian Society for Yad Vashem's memorial service, held Sept. 17 at the Yad Vashem
Holocaust memorial in Earl Bales Park. Commemorative wreaths were also laid. Rabbi
Philip Scheim and Cantor Marshall Loomer officiated.   [Frances Kraft photo]

A very special and solemn moment I shared with my grandson Blake in
September 2000 at the Canadian Society for Yad Vashem Holocaust
Memorial Site, where we lit a commemorative candle to honour those
who perished. See page 151. Courtesy of the *Canadian Jewish News* and
photographer Frances Kraft.

Spending quality time reading to Blake (right) and Cole, 1997.

From the office to the field to enjoy Jared's soccer game.

One of many happy moments with my granddaughter, Madison, circa early 2000s.

Cuddling with my youngest grandson, Harrison.

Celebrating Gretka's eightieth birthday in Bermuda in 1998.

With Joseph Ecker (my maternal first cousin) at my first family reunion in 2009. See page 152.

With Ruth and Jack Weiss's son, Manny, at a family reunion in Toronto in June 2011. He graciously brought an album of old family photographs.

With our close friends Toby and Saul Feldberg. See page 118.

With Eddie and Valerie Rosenberg in Israel.

With my love, Grace Lindover.

At my ninetieth/ninety-first birthday evening. Back row, left to right: Ellen, David (Grace's son; Ellen and David's daughter, Kate, not pictured), Jamie (Grace's eldest son), Laura, Cory, Sean (Jamie and Laura's sons), Caity (Sean's fiancée). Front row: Me, Grace, Frances (Grace's sister).

In Toronto with Eva and her two daughters, Annik (left) and Jessica (far right).

In a Bedouin tent during Blake's bar mitzvah at Eretz Bereshit (Genesis Land) in Israel, March 2007. See page 159.

13

THE 1990s AND BEYOND

I N THIS SECOND half of my life, my business flourished and there were many significant moments that today I look back on and cherish. One took place in April 1994, when my friend and client Saul Feldberg, of Global Upholstery Company, and Hank Rosenbaum, co-president of Canadian Jewish Holocaust Survivors and Descendants, invited me to join them and several hundred survivors from around the world to attend the Papal Concert to Commemorate the Shoah. Pope John Paul II, who was Polish, was the first non-Italian pope in history, and this initiative was the first time the Vatican had officially commemorated the murder of six million Jews in World War II. Among the dignitaries was Rav Elio Toaff, the Chief Rabbi of Rome. Today it is considered one of the most significant events in Catholic-Jewish relations. I remember sitting with Grace in the Paul VI Audience Hall at the Vatican and the powerful emotions I felt when the Pope said, "The walls of this hall have no limits. The victims, fathers, mothers, brothers, sisters, and friends are here with you. They are with us. They will never be forgotten."

Later, I stood in line to meet the Pope. When he shook my hand, he asked in Polish where I was from. I replied in Czech and he understood me, Polish and Czech being similar enough to make that possible. It was quite a humbling experience.

Two years later, on Monday, May 13, 1996, I was invited to join several other survivors in Ontario's Legislative Building at Queen's Park. Grace was with me, as well as Audrey and Alexandria; Audrey's husband, Graham; and his parents, Valerie and Eddie. Attorney General Charles Harnick said, "Without the memories of the Holocaust survivors and their families, this horror might be allowed to fade into the pages of history, which it must never be allowed to do if we are to ensure that it never happens again. As time passes, it is going to be more difficult to convey to future generations what happened in Eastern Europe during the Second World War."

It was another moving ceremony and I have the framed document with which I was presented hanging in my office. It reads:

In Recognition and Appreciation
THOMAS SIMON NEWMAN
Holocaust Survivor

As we gather to observe the 51st Anniversary of the end of the Second World War and the liberation of Europe, we honour you for your extraordinary contribution to the province of Ontario.

Your achievements were forged from suffering that few can comprehend, but that all must remember. We can never forget the sacrifice of those who perished in the Holocaust, nor the strength of those who survived. You bore the unbearable, and not even great loss could prevent you from giving of yourself to others and enriching the depth and integrity of our province.

I salute you today for your profound place in the collective memory of our society. Please accept my warm, best wishes for a long and fulfilling future.

The Honourable Michael D. Harris
Premier of Ontario

In yet another ceremony, this time in September 2000, my family joined me at the Canadian Society for Yad Vashem Holocaust Memorial Site at Toronto's Earl Bales Park. I had arranged for the names of my parents and siblings (Alexander, Rosalia, Isaac, Artur, Friderika, Ludmila, Irena, and Morris) to be inscribed on one of the eight marble Walls of Remembrance. There is a picture, published in the *Canadian Jewish News*, of my six-year-old grandson Blake and me lighting one of six commemorative candles. These kinds of events remind us that we must "never forget."

DO YOU REMEMBER, back in 1953, when I had a surprise visit from my first cousins, Ruth and Jack Weiss? They had returned to Toronto a couple of times in the 1970s. Early in 2009, I received a phone call from Manny, their son. Ruth had died, but Manny and his sisters, Lenore and Doris, remembered their mother talking about a relative in Toronto, reminding them not to forget about him. Manny asked one of his sisters for their mother's address book and was happy to find my name and phone number and called me. We spoke for a while, and then he invited me to attend a family reunion on a long weekend in June at a resort in the Pocono Mountains in Pennsylvania. I was excited to plan this trip and meet my cousins.

When Grace and I arrived at the Skytop Lodge, it was a rainy day and we were not sure what to expect. We were sitting at a table in the dining room wondering how we would identify my relatives from other guests, when a couple walked over to us and introduced themselves. It turned out to be my second cousin Lee Ecker and his wife, Bari. We chatted for a few minutes about family connections and then Lee and Bari led us to another room where at least fifty heads turned to look at me. They were all family and everyone later said that I wore a big smile and tears glistened in my eyes. Everyone was happy to meet me; in fact, they made quite a fuss and I ended up talking to many relatives from my mother's side of the family. There is a picture of me with Joseph Ecker, my mother's brother's son (first cousin to me!), who was quite elderly and in a wheelchair at that time. Sadly, he died not long after the reunion. I am grateful that I got to meet him.

A couple of years later, another reunion was scheduled, this time in Toronto. The out-of-town family members stayed at the InterContinental Hotel on Bloor Street West and I was able to mingle with all these Eckers again. It was an opportunity for me to spend more time with them and introduce them to my children and grandchildren. We were a large group, with my cousins attending with their families as well. My daughters were thrilled to meet the Eckers and to feel part of a larger family. They became friendly with Lenore's daughters, Shari and Amy, and I'm delighted that they have kept in touch. The reunion weekend was filled with sightseeing activities, and we had a big dinner at the hotel. There were speeches and I thoroughly enjoyed seeing our large family tree laid out on a table for us to look at and to which we added our names. My cousins also brought family photo albums so I could see pictures of some of my mother's siblings who had moved to the US before World War II. The reunion ended on a beautiful summer evening with Audrey and Graham hosting a barbecue at their home. For someone who had lost his family, it was overwhelming and exhilarating at the same time.

Speaking of relatives, in the fall of 2012, Audrey, Alexandria, Grace, and I went to New Jersey to visit my cousin Alex Ecker. When planning this trip, Alex's daughter Ruth told my daughters that there had to be one condition: that we not talk at all about the war or the camps. Alex never spoke about the past, not the war years. His children knew little about his horrific experiences. When we arrived, Alex and I were happy to see each other and we had a very enjoyable visit chatting a bit about our childhood in Vojnatina and otherwise about our lives after the war. Alex was thriving and owned an income property. Alex and I went for a drive on our own to see the property and have some one-on-one time.

Back at their house, we talked about our families and really enjoyed visiting with Alex and his wife, Marilyn. We had lunches and dinners together along with their daughters, Francine and Ruth, and granddaughters, Jacqueline and Melissa. Once again, my daughters were happy to meet their second cousins and expand our small family. It was great to see Alex again. In the years that followed, Marilyn became ill and sadly passed away. Alex has had some health issues as well so we haven't seen each other since. I hope we will be able to visit again.

I cannot leave out a special birthday. For my eightieth, a celebration was organized for a Friday in early April; Graham arranged for an event space and quite a gathering took place. Along with my entire family, the party included Grace's sons, Jamie (with his wife, Laura) and David (with his wife, Ellen), Grace's sister, Frances (with her husband, Stan), and Graham's parents, with whom I have always been very close. Best of all, Bobek and Gretka's daughter, Eva, and her daughter, Jessica, arrived from Calgary; as well, their son, Chuck, and his wife, Diane, flew in from

Bermuda, where they live. At the last minute, I mentioned it to my firm's partners, and one of them, Elliot, was able to join us with his wife, Maura. It was wonderfully catered and they hired an accordionist and a violinist who played everything from classical music to Jewish and Hungarian songs. I remember smiling and clapping along and even dancing with Eva.

Audrey and Alexandria had prepared a poem and they alternated reciting the verses, much to my delight. (The Lexus refers to a car I won in a draw. I had never won anything before and at first, I wasn't sure about keeping it, but I must say I am happy I did.)

1930 in Vojnatina our dad came to be
The most handsome blond, green-eyed boy you ever
did see
Born to Alexander and Rosalia in this town
He became a Neumann, he is now renowned

Unbelievably, he drank milk straight from the goat
[much laughter greeted this line]
Now it is only lactose-free that enters his throat
He was one of seven children before the war
He has overcome such grief and left that shore

To Canada he came, and Toronto it would be
Thankfully for us because he created our family
Young, charismatic, handsome, with lots of hair
[more laughter]
He charmed the women with his style and flair

The hair has thinned, but really, who cares?
The charm remains no matter what he wears
We all know that it is a shirt with pants, not jeans
We gave that a shot, but we gave up in our teens

From American cars to Lexus since the big win
We all love to tease him and see that big grin
Fine taste and deserving of only the best
Where to dine? Having tablecloths, that is the test

Being messy, have a blemish, oh don't worry
Before Dad comes, clean and get concealer in a hurry
Two daughters, then grandchildren, he did create
All that he accomplished is nothing short of great

It is his grandchildren who truly fill his heart
And in their lives, he plays a huge part
As a papa, he is definitely number one
They are the luckiest kids under the sun

You've always been a very special dad
To have you for life we couldn't be more glad
We know you're busy all day doing tax
But tonight is your chance to just sit back and relax

Eighty years is a milestone and why
we're so happy to celebrate with you
Wishing you health and happiness
now and always, WE LOVE YOU

I am not one for lengthy speeches, and I am certainly not a comedian, so I kept it short and sweet. I

thanked Grace, Audrey, Alexandria, and Graham for arranging the party, and then I touched the front of my head and said, "If you're bald in the front, you're a thinker." Moving my hand to the back of my head, I continued, "If you're bald in the back, you're sexy." Then, glancing over at Graham, who shaves his head, I said, "If you're bald all over, you *think* you're sexy." The room erupted in laughter and applause and the party continued into the night.

Our family celebrated every event, from birthdays and graduations to my grandsons' bar mitzvahs and my granddaughter's bat mitzvah, plus those of Grace's grandchildren. A regular visitor was Gretka and Bobek's daughter, Eva, who came at least once a year and always stayed at my house. Later, her daughters, Jessica and Annik, started making regular visits to Toronto as well. We went to Ottawa to attend Annik's wedding to Adam in 2016; in 2020, Annik brought baby Thomas to visit us. I fussed over the baby, so the family called us "Big Thomas" and "Little Thomas." Eva's brother, Chuck, and his wife, Diane, also came to visit a few times a year from their home in Bermuda. Their son, Rhys, is a lawyer in Toronto and we occasionally have lunch together. They are all very important and close members of our family.

Still, of all the many family dinners and visits, two specific celebrations stand out because they involved extended periods of family time. In March 2007, Audrey's son, Blake, became my first grandchild to reach the age of thirteen. We decided to celebrate his bar mitzvah by extending March Break to two weeks spent in Israel. A fairly large group of us came from Toronto. Flying in from Australia were Graham's uncle and aunt Bert and Pauline, as well as a cousin, Anton, and his wife, Sharron. We were also joined by Graham's uncle and aunt Lenny and Batya, and their children Yael, Jonathan, and Zviki along with their families. (They live in Israel and thus didn't have far to travel.)

I loved this trip and the time we all had together. We mostly travelled in a rented bus that could accommodate everyone along with an Israeli tour guide. From Tel Aviv, we drove to the old city of Jerusalem and explored the Jewish Quarter, the Cardo, and the Wailing Wall where, as is customary, we said a prayer and put a note on which some wishes or prayers had been written into the cracks of the wall.

We also visited Yad Vashem, Israel's impressive Holocaust memorial located on the western side of Mount Herzl. In addition to its role as a research institute, it is home to the Holocaust History Museum and a Children's Memorial, which commemorates the approximately 1.5 million children and young people, like my brothers and sisters, who died at the hands of the Nazis. The main hall is covered in mirrors reflecting the light from five candles, and the names of the dead children, including their ages and places of death, are recited on a tape loop that would take three months to listen to from beginning to end. To be there with my grandchildren, all of whom were the ages of many of the victims, was a solemn and profoundly emotional experience.

Over the two weeks, we visited the Knesset, the national legislature of Israel, and the Supreme Court building. Later we went to Beit Guvrin National Park where we explored the underground caves and took part in an archaeological dig.

Finally, on the day of Blake's bar mitzvah, March 15, we departed Jerusalem on our bus. The ceremony was supposed to take place at Masada, the ancient fortification built by Herod the Great on top of a mountain on the eastern edge of the Judaean Desert, overlooking the Dead Sea. Unfortunately, a stretch of rainy weather had left the road up the mountain flooded so we had to change our plans.

Instead, we drove to Eretz Bereshit, or Genesis Land as it is known in English, in the Judaean Desert on the way to the Dead Sea. It is where Abraham and the other patriarchs were believed to have lived. The idea is for visitors to experience a bit of what life was like in Biblical times so we were first greeted by Eliezer, Abraham's manservant, who led us, along with his train of camels, to Abraham's tent, where Abraham himself greeted us at his Bedouin tent. They were, of course, actors, but the overall effect was marvellous, especially when we were given traditional Bedouin garb to wear.

The bimah, the traditional table on which the Torah sits, had been set up in the tent along with tables for all the guests. At the appointed time, I watched proudly as my grandson Blake read an assigned portion of the Haftorah, lessons from the Prophets. Both of Blake's grandfathers—myself and Graham's father, Eddie—received the honour of an aliyah, so we both stood at the bimah and recited a blessing from the Torah. At the end, Blake's brother and sister, Cole and Maddie, sang a hymn, "Adon Olam," and everyone threw candies into the air and yelled Mazel Tov before singing "Siman Tov u'Mazel Tov." And what a feast we had while at Genesis Land: vegetables, hummus with freshly baked pita, date honey chicken, meatballs and rice, dried fruits...

The combination of where we were and that it was my first grandson's bar mitzvah made this a truly memorable trip for me.

It was not the only special bar mitzvah celebration. In December 2014, the entire family flew via Miami to St. Thomas in the US Virgin Islands, staying at the Frenchman's Reef Marriott Resort for a week. The occasion was the bar mitzvah for Alexandria's son Harrison. It was wonderful being together around the pool and for meals in such a beautiful place. We had an extra special outdoor lunch and dinner with speeches to celebrate the occasion. There was some time for shopping and exploring the island and everyone chose what they wanted to do.

The highlight, though, was the bar mitzvah, held on December 27. We gathered at the St. Thomas Synagogue, which is the second oldest synagogue in the western hemisphere and one of only five in the world with a sand floor. It symbolizes the Jews who had to secretly practise their religion in cellars and used sand to muffle the sound. The synagogue was originally built in 1796 by a small congregation of Sephardic Jews, many of whom had arrived on St. Thomas escaping religious intolerance in Spain and Portugal. A fire destroyed the original building in 1831 but two years later it was rebuilt into the beautiful structure we entered that day. The Torah ark, made of local mahogany and containing six Torahs, is on one wall, with the tebah, or pulpit, across from it. The seven-branch menorah dates back to the eleventh century. The centre of the chamber is divided by four columns and there are rows of bench-style pews. The overall effect is intimate and profoundly spiritual.

To my surprise, the Rabbi, Ron Herstik, was the son of Holocaust survivors from Czechoslovakia. After the service, we all made a circle around Harrison and Rabbi Herstik allowed me to hold one Torah with special significance. It had been looted by Nazis from a Czech synagogue in the town of Budyne nad Ohri. Hitler had told his military leaders to destroy the synagogues but save the scrolls and silver for his intended "Museum of the Extinct Race" once all Jews were dead. This Torah had a Nazi inventory number on it. During the Liberation, Allied soldiers collected all the scrolls and returned them, and this one ended up here in St. Thomas.

As I held it, I realized that this Torah, and others like it, represented the failure of Hitler's mad and inhuman ambitions. It symbolized how the Jewish people continue to survive and, in my case, how I miraculously walked out of Buchenwald in 1945 and began a long journey to the happiness and satisfaction I know today.

[TOP] Dinner with Chuck (Bobek and Gretka's son) and Chuck's son, Rhys, in Toronto.

[MIDDLE] Hard at work in the first office on Adelaide at Spadina (circa mid-1950s).

[BOTTOM] At my desk in the office, where I still spend a lot of my time.

[TOP LEFT] With Martin Sversky, my friend and business partner since 1966.

[TOP RIGHT] With my son-in-law, Graham, who has been a fixture in the family as Audrey's husband, as a father to Blake, Cole, and Madison, and as the son I never had.

[MIDDLE] In New Jersey with my cousin Alex in 2012.

[BOTTOM] With my American cousins at the family reunion in Toronto in June 2011. Left to right: Larry Ecker, Lee Ecker, me, Sidney Ecker, Manny Weiss, Lenore Levine, and Howard Ecker.

[TOP] A family celebration for both my ninetieth and ninety-first birthdays that I'll never forget, July 18, 2021. Back row: Blake, Graham, Audrey, Alexandria, Madison, Cole, Jared. Front row: Me and Grace. (Harrison not pictured.)

[BOTTOM] "Big Thomas" meets "Little Thomas" (Annik's son and Eva's grandson) in 2020.

Harrison and Jared at my home.

Wearing the special hats made up for my birthday celebration—"Tommy's 90th/91st"—with Blake, Madison, and Cole.

My loving daughters.

A line from a poem of Audrey's: "You are my hero, my wonderful dad, /
To be your daughter, I couldn't be more glad."

A line from Alexandria's tribute: "As a teacher, I have often asked my students to write about their hero. Mine is an easy choice: my dad."

Audrey and Graham arrive at Auschwitz during the March of the Living on May 2, 2019. See the Afterword.

Audrey tells my story while the March of the Living participants and survivors listen.

Audrey takes me on an emotional tour of the grounds of Auschwitz using FaceTime. This was my first time seeing Auschwitz since I was a prisoner in the camp.

Listening to the speeches during the family reunion held in Toronto in June 2011.

AFTERWORD: MARCH OF THE LIVING

BY AUDREY NEWMAN

Over the years, I became increasingly interested in my father's experience and in the movement to ensure that the Holocaust is not forgotten. To truly understand the Holocaust, I thought I should go to where the atrocities had occurred. It is critical to stand where evil took place and to realize how close the European cities and towns were to each other. It is difficult to comprehend that people living near the concentration camps were completely unaware of what was happening on the other side of those fences.

I had been thinking about going on the March of the Living for a number of years, ever since I had first heard about it. It's an annual program that brings students and adults to Poland, where they see the remnants of the Holocaust. Participants first spend a week visiting locations of Nazi persecution, such as the Warsaw Ghetto, various synagogues, and the extermination camp, Treblinka. Then on Holocaust and Heroism Remembrance Day, Yom HaShoah, which is either in April or May, thousands of people gather in the town of Oswiecim to take part in a three-kilometre silent march from Auschwitz to Birkenau. These camps were the two largest sections of the Nazi concentration camp complex. From there, many go on to Israel to observe Yom HaZikaron, Israel's Remembrance Day, and Yom HaAtzmaut, Israel's Independence Day.

My dad had talked to Madison about going on her March of the Living trip in 2016. At first he was interested in going, but then he became indecisive about participating. I think the idea of visiting Auschwitz was a bit overwhelming for him, especially at eighty-six. When he finally declined, he said, "I don't need to go. I think of every member of my family every day." Madison understood and spoke to him on the day of the march. I knew he would not go on my trip as one of the survivors, so I suggested that we could use modern technology to allow him to virtually accompany me.

I flew out with a number of others from the Canadian delegation on April 29 to arrive in Krakow. We got there a day early and benefitted from a good night's sleep before the tour began. The next day we explored Kazimierz, the Jewish Quarter, staring in wonder at the stunning architecture of the Old Synagogue and Oskar Schindler's factory where he employed and saved the lives of 1,200 Jews.

That night, I had a long phone conversation with my dad in which he told me more details about his experience than I had heard before. He said it was just good luck that Hungary had occupied his part of Czechoslovakia, because Czech Jews were sent to the camps much earlier than those in Hungary. He said, "I remember my parents saying that the Messiah had come." This turned out to be too optimistic, as his family was still rounded up and sent to the ghetto in Uzhorod before being put on the cattle cars bound for Auschwitz. He said he has never forgotten seeing his mother holding baby Morris in her arms, unable to feed him. And, once they reached Auschwitz, how he had held on to a faint hope that his mother, sisters, and the baby were alive even though he knew it was more likely that they had been sent to the gas chambers.

For the first time, he told me in detail about his father being pulled out of the line when being assessed for fitness and how his father gave him a piece of bread that he had saved. He told me, "We used to take off our shirts and walk in front of the guards with our arms held out to display our tattoos. My dad looked very frail and he was called out of the line." As he watched his father being led away, my dad knew he was going to be executed. It was such a gut-wrenching moment that we both broke down crying. I felt so sad, for everything he had been through and lost, and also guilty, wondering whether I was dredging up too many memories that my dad might have preferred to never revisit. I felt I had to try to cheer him up, so I told him to think about the beautiful family he had created, the wonderful life he had given us, and all of his adoring grandchildren. He responded, "I am okay. I am so grateful for my family and proud of all of you." That night, I hoped he could get to sleep without being haunted by our conversation.

We were divided into two buses and each bus had a survivor who travelled with us. On our first day I met Max Eisen, a Hungarian Jew who was also deported to Auschwitz around the same time as my father. After retiring, he became an active speaker and educator and he volunteers at Toronto's Friends of Simon Wiesenthal Center for Holocaust Studies and the Neuberger Holocaust Education Centre.

The survivor on the other bus was Nate Leipciger, a Polish Jew who spent time with his father in the notorious Sosnowiec Ghetto and was then transferred to Auschwitz-Birkenau and other concentration camps before ending up in Dachau when American soldiers arrived. Nate and his father survived and were sponsored by an uncle to come to Toronto. I would get to know both remarkable men over the days that followed.

Once we had arrived at Oswiecim, I felt a chill despite the sunny weather. Standing on the tracks that led into Auschwitz—the ones that brought train after train after train, each cattle car crammed with Jews destined for back-breaking labour, or to succumb to the diseases commonplace in any concentration camp, or to face immediate death—I imagined my dad and his family stumbling out of a cattle car, disoriented, being ordered in loud, nasty voices to line up. I imagined how frightening that must have been. My dad had just turned fourteen.

Today, grass has grown, softening the appearance somewhat, but at the time, there was none, just bare earth that often turned to mud. I walked toward the remnants of the gas chambers and crematoria. To think, my dad had been somewhere else, being prepared for work, while his mother, three sisters, and baby brother were in the gas chamber. I walked inside a gas chamber and thought about how Zyklon B hydrogen cyanide pellets were dropped through holes into the chamber. It was incomprehensible that human beings did these things. I felt sick to my stomach.

The tour took us around Auschwitz. I saw a wall where prisoners had been lined up to watch as fellow prisoners, accused of one misdemeanour or another, were shot or hanged. I also saw various kinds of barracks and the crude remains of what passed for latrines—holes in the ground spaced quite closely together. I was quiet, taking it all in, imagining that this is where my dad had walked, slept, and suffered.

That night, at our hotel, our trip leaders organized a celebration for Yom HaShoah, Holocaust and Heroism Remembrance Day. The experience of the survivors dancing with us arm-in-arm, and the way everyone treated them as honoured guests, made me so wish my dad was with me. I wanted him to be honoured and to be among the other survivors. I ended up dancing with Max Eisen, who reminded me of my dad.

On May 2, I FaceTimed with my dad. As he sat in his home in Toronto, I showed him the massive crowd: 10,000 people from fifty-two countries, many carrying flags or banners. He was amazed at the sea of people and told me he felt happy that I was there honouring him and his family. Again, thanks to the miracle of FaceTime, I could show him how I placed a plaque with the names of his family on the train tracks. "I feel like I am there with you," he said. "It is a mitzvah what you are doing. You are honouring my family and all the Jews who were killed, who should always be remembered."

Later, I gave him a tour of Auschwitz, the first time he'd seen it since the war. When I showed him one set of brick barracks, he said they didn't look like the ones he had been in. So, I walked over toward another set of barracks, showing him everything along the way. He recognized the guard towers and asked me if the twelve-foot-high barbed-wire fence was there. "Yes," I said as we both stared at it, the electrical insulators lining the concrete posts. He was quiet for a bit after that.

When I approached a set of wooden barracks, he said, "That is where I was! Are those really them?" I explained that the Nazis had destroyed them, but these were exact replicas that had been built. He recognized the one-storey structures right away as the ones he had been in.

It was another highly emotional day. I told him many times how much I loved him, and that because of his will to survive and his hope for a future, I was able to be here and show him all of this. I was able to bear witness in a meaningful way, both by being there and having the privilege of learning from my father.

Over the course of a couple of days I talked to Max Eisen and Nate Leipciger about their books. Max's book, *By Chance Alone: A Remarkable True Story of Courage and Survival at Auschwitz*, became a national bestseller and Nate's memoir was called *The Weight of Freedom*. It takes courage to write this type of memoir and I admired them for it. I had my copy of Max's book with me, which he signed. I was thinking at that moment that my dad's story should also be written, because every Holocaust survivor's story is important and adds to the historical record.

Most of the people in the Canadian contingent of this March of the Living tour had grandparents who were survivors. I met only a few people whose parents were survivors. One day, I was asked if I would like to speak, to tell my father's story. I asked if I could do it in front of the whole group. It had been too busy a day to have managed it at Auschwitz, but we agreed it would take place when we visited another concentration camp, Majdanek, on the outskirts of the Polish town of Lublin.

That evening I wrote and rewrote my short presentation, knowing I had to get it just right. I spoke to my father and read him what I had prepared, and he was both moved and encouraging.

As usual, our entire group gathered, in this case at a monument at the gates to the camp. Everyone wore headphones, normally used to listen to our guide but today I held the microphone. I admit that I was nervous, and once or twice I choked up, but everyone listened intently and was very supportive. Afterwards, people hugged me and said it was a powerful story and that I told it well. Some were crying. Graham and a few friends recorded it on their phones, so I was able to show it to my father when I returned home. It made him very emotional, but he seemed quite happy that I had done it.

What a week. What a roller coaster of emotions. I knew I would need time to process it all. At the closing ceremony, we gathered with young people who had been on their own tour. Various people spoke about the importance of remembering and of Holocaust education. We sang the Kaddish. Many people suggested I should encourage my dad to become a speaker, to give presentations as a survivor who knows and remembers the horrors of the Holocaust. I knew my modest father, who did not like having attention on him, would be unlikely to do that, but perhaps he would do it in writing.

Speaking to my father on the phone one night from Poland, I mentioned it. He said, "Maybe. We can discuss it when you get home." Knowing my father very well, I was not surprised by this response; I knew he would need time to process the idea. When I got home, I began planting the seed. I told him that everyone on the trip thought his story was important and needed to be told. "This is a great way to teach people. This is also a way to honour your family," I said. "A young generation won't necessarily remember. This is how people will learn about what happened during the Holocaust."

My father firmly believes in tolerance and the good in people and that to incite hatred is dangerous. He decided to tell his story, with these ideas in mind and with the love and encouragement of his entire family.

EPILOGUE

SEEING AUSCHWITZ THROUGH my daughter's eyes stirred up many emotions. It took me back to a time I have mainly tried to forget. There was the camp, now a memorial so no one forgets the horrors that happened, except now grass has grown and you can hear birds—symbols of how much has changed. Seeing it also reminded me that one of the reasons I survived is that I never lost hope—the hope to live freely and enjoy these pleasantries of nature that only existed outside the camp. I love spending time outdoors and am happiest sitting in the backyard of my home.

I wrote this book out of a need to tell my own story of survival and also to honour the memory, and the irreparable loss, of my parents, siblings, and other relations. I believe that those who survived the Holocaust owe it to future generations to put on record as much evidence as possible of the Nazi's reign of terror. Just as I never take for granted the wonderful freedoms I have enjoyed here in Canada, the world must never forget that the Holocaust began as the loss of a series of small freedoms. We cannot be bystanders when freedoms are threatened.

Some of the memories I had to confront were brutal and painful, but I am relieved to say that others—especially those involving my life after Liberation in Prague and then in my new home in Canada, and particularly those involving my family—were happy, joyous ones. They represent a tangible symbol of the hope in my heart that has always been with me.

I will not be here forever, but this book will be a document to remind my daughters and my grandchildren and, I hope, their children and generations beyond of what I lived through. They will become the custodians of these memories and the spirit of hope they contain.

On April 6, 2020, I turned ninety just after the COVID-19 pandemic arrived in Canada and we experienced the first lockdown. My children and grandchildren surprised me by standing in my driveway holding signs with letters spelling out "Happy Birthday." We could not hug or be close together around the dining table, but from a distance we took photos, toasted with plastic cups, and it was, in spite of the restrictions, a lot of fun.

These restrictions, as difficult and inconvenient as they are for everyone, did not trigger memories of the camps because, after all, I was experiencing the lockdown in a free country, in the comfort of my home, where Grace and I have our own company and all the luxuries one could ask for, and where I can at least see my children and grandchildren at a distance. Of course, Grace and I would like to get out more often, and travel, but that time will come. I felt more comfortable when we both got the first dose of a vaccine, so I am hopeful this pandemic, too, will end.

Lately, I began returning to my accounting firm, masked and distanced from those who are present, and mainly sitting in my large, private office. People ask me, "Why do you do this? You don't have to work any longer." The answer is simple: I love what I do and I have such great clients and colleagues to be around. It adds significant meaning to my life.

Shortly after my birthday, in April 2020, I needed some minor surgery on my back for a melanoma. This was done at Humber River Hospital by a very nice surgeon, Dr. Romy Ahluwalia. Audrey told him that the last time I had required surgery on my back was when I was fifteen years old and in a concentration camp during the war. When Dr. Ahluwalia realized I was a survivor, he was impressed. He said he was so honoured to meet me, that he had so much respect for survivors of the Holocaust. He was a very kind man from the beginning, but he made sure to make me feel very important and cared for. Unlike that time in Buchenwald in 1945, I was getting the best of twenty-first-century medical treatment in a modern hospital.

Ultimately, I feel fortunate every day to know that I am here in a safe country, where my children have been able to grow and flourish, and my hope now, rather than for my own survival, is for the continued success of my grandchildren as they choose their respective paths in life. I am extremely proud of all of them and feel very blessed.

One summer weekend, before the pandemic, I visited with friends in their backyard. On a table, there was a bowl with honey in it. Bees were going into it and then could not get out. Some were struggling; others were already dead. It reminded me that there have been times in this world when people have deliberately done that to other people. I hope it never happens again. It is easier to be friendly than to be unfriendly. It is easier to love than to hate.

TRIBUTES
FROM FAMILY
MEMBERS

GRACE LINDOVER'S TRIBUTE

Tom and I were fortunate to find each other later in life and we have had a very, very happy time together. We have had an active social life and enjoyed travelling—including a picturesque cruise to Alaska, and several trips to Israel. We have been fortunate to experience many memorable trips together with friends and family. Spending time with all of our children and grandchildren is always precious time for us. Tom is a kind, generous man who had lost so much during the war. When he suddenly reunited with an extended family of Eckers, he was overjoyed, and I was equally happy to be involved and share in his joy. It is exciting that he decided to tell his remarkable story so that the world will remember what it means to have hope. We are all so proud of him and know that this book will be cherished by so many.

AUDREY NEWMAN'S TRIBUTE

You are my hero, my wonderful dad
To be your daughter, I couldn't be more glad

You have lived through a lot, we can't imagine the scope
How incredible you are to persevere and live life with
hope

You came to Canada, to Toronto, in 1948
Hard-working and so determined to do something great

That you have accomplished, your own firm, doing
what you love
The dedication and work ethic is simply over and above

We joke about words that you say in your own way
Such as blueberry, cookie, figure, and then, of course,
Tuesday

I love that you laugh at your own jokes with a grin
upon your face
And can spontaneously sing or dance no matter the place

We share a love of tennis and playing together was so
much fun
But one thing you sure love more than me is sitting in
the sun

We share a love of fashion, but you are more finely
dressed
A suit, white shirt, and tie, always perfectly pressed

Handsome, kind, smart, humble are words that
describe you best
And the way you carry yourself, living life with such zest

A better role model for us there could never be
I am so very thankful, all I can say is lucky me

There is nothing in this world, that for you I wouldn't do
Words just cannot express how immensely I love you

I have written poems for my dad on several special occasions and publishing his life story is certainly one of those. What is a special occasion for my dad? Anything that brings his family together. When he sits at the head of the table for a family dinner or holiday, such as Passover, he smiles and takes it all in. Passovers are an especially happy memory for me because I love to watch my dad being the proud patriarch. He gets everyone to be quiet so that he can listen to family members, especially his grandchildren, read parts of the seder. He truly appreciates being able to carry on these traditions with us.

I also love our daily conversations during which there are usually some laughs. Lately we have been having a lot of fun as he teaches me Slovak words and phrases. I love hearing him laugh when I incorporate them into our conversations. I feel lucky that we also get to spend a lot of time together, and one recent trip to Florida stands out in my mind. We spent a week going for walks on the boardwalk by the beach, sitting by the pool, and trying different restaurants for dinner. My dad has taught me that the most important thing in life is family.

I am so proud and happy that my dad decided to write his story, both for his family and other readers, as he has an incredible story to tell that serves as an important lesson on living life after tremendous loss.

GRAHAM ROSENBERG'S TRIBUTE

What an honour to be the son you never had. And what an honour to know you the way I do, and the lessons I've learned. From the depths of depravity and loss unimaginable, you have taught everyone around you the most important of life lessons. Life is all about the choices you make. You've chosen to live your life honourably, positively, and resolutely, with your special brand of humour. For that, you have my utmost respect and admiration.

We have a shared passion for sports, especially tennis (not so much baseball, your favourite). And you have certainly earned and embraced the best that life has to offer. I'm thinking of your penchant for restaurants with white cloth service (of which I'm quite fond), as well as tailored suits, fine shirts, and Hermès ties (I can do without ties). All this certainly brings out your European roots.

But as we know, life is about family and friends, of which you have many. Your fierce loyalty is unwavering and your ability to accept whatever life presents, without judging, and of always seeing the good side of bad, make it easy to be around you and are the reasons for all the love you receive in return.

Not only have you been an amazing father-in-law, but a wonderful friend for the last four decades. I'm looking forward to many more.

BLAKE ROSENBERG'S TRIBUTE

One of my favourite memories with Papa that I'll always cherish may sound simple to some, but it left a lasting impact on me. As a kid, I would ride my bike over to his house, often with very little notice (one of the benefits of living so close to him), and he would have chips and ketchup waiting for me, one of my favourite snacks. He and I would always have long chats at the dinner table, or outside depending on the weather, and I'd always stay a lot longer than I had originally planned. We would talk about sports, school, and whatever else was going on in our lives. I will always value the advice he gave me about my future career and how to live life to the fullest, but mostly just the quality time we spent together. Papa's face would always light up when I visited, which made it all the more worthwhile.

In my later years, I've come to find out that my grandfather was, and still technically is, the ladies' man of the family. I definitely will never forget all of our chats about girls, and his sense of humour about that area of my life. It's quite rare that someone in their mid-twenties can talk about their personal life in detail with their grandfather and have him actually understand and speak to you about it like a friend. This was especially true when he told me not to wear my ripped jeans on a date because, he would joke, the girl would think I can't afford to buy new jeans.

Aside from all the memories with Papa, one of his primary impacts on all of us is that he is someone we can all look up to. As this book has shown, he has endured significant trauma in his life but has overcome it with immense success. With resilience, determination, and hard work, he was able to survive one of the darkest times in human history, move to Canada, start a family, and grow a successful business. It is very motivating, as much as it is admirable, because it makes me feel like I can do anything I set my mind to. He has shown that no matter the obstacle, it can be overcome.

COLE ROSENBERG'S TRIBUTE

It is difficult to think about just one moment that captures everything there is to say about Papa. For a generally quiet man, he has taught me and our family many significant lessons, far more than he would ever know. He is a stellar role model and leads by example, always in his interest of ensuring his family is taken care of. He is truly admirable, especially since he has been through more than anyone could begin to imagine, yet you would never know that from the outside looking in. This is an incredible achievement in itself.

I have so many great memories from growing up just around the corner from Papa. We were incredibly lucky to have him so close and to spend as much time with him as we did. He is a staple in our home videos from when my brother, my sister, and I were kids and it is clear to see how much fun we had with him.

When I think of Papa, the first thing that comes to mind is the look of happiness on his face when he sits at the head of the table during countless Shabbat dinners and holiday celebrations at his house. Toward the end of every dinner, I would go around to his end of the table to talk to him. He always asked tons of questions about whatever sports event I had that week, what was going on at school, or essentially anything else that my siblings or I were up to. To this day, he still only wants to hear about us, instead of talking about himself.

Papa has always told me I work too hard and need to take more time off, which is something coming from him since I have watched him work tirelessly as long as I've known him, even recently when many have asked him to take more days away from the office. It is not in his character to slow down, and I have learned from that and strived for the same work ethic from a very young age. I recently spoke to Papa about a new job opportunity in New York, and although he said it is difficult for him to see one of his grandchildren move away, he is extremely happy for me and knows that I "will be a very important man there one day." I certainly hope to make him proud.

Papa is a prime example of what can happen through hard work, dedication, and perseverance. He has taught me that there is no way around hard work and that if you set your mind to something, you can achieve it. He has also instilled in me the lesson that there are no excuses or handouts, in life—you must earn everything. He is a true story of resilience and bravery and I am extremely proud to be his grandson.

MADDIE ROSENBERG'S TRIBUTE

There really aren't enough words to adequately describe my papa. He is the hardest worker I know and has always been incredibly supportive of all of us. As a kid, I was always so excited when Papa would babysit as we always had so much fun together. Instead of reading us a book before bed, he often created his own stories to tell us and they were unique and funny. One story that changed each time he told it was "the kook and the frog." He never failed to make us laugh and continues to do so today. He also loves to make up songs to perform for us.

Another fun thing we did together when I was younger was play with my dolls. He would run up and down the driveway with me saying, "Don't fall down," in his playful way, while I pushed the dolls in a stroller. This became a trademark for him and whenever we would do anything that made him nervous, even just walking up the steps to his front door, he would say, "Don't fall down."

I didn't talk to Papa much about his childhood until I was older because I wanted to avoid upsetting him. He did share some details with me when I asked, and that made me want to learn more and inspired me to go on the March of the Living. Leading up to the trip, I had to interview a survivor and tell the group whom I was marching for. During the days I spent interviewing Papa, he expressed that although it made him emotional, he was proud of me for going. On the day of the march from Auschwitz to Birkenau, I FaceTimed Papa to tell him how the day was. He told me again how proud of me he was and to always remember that I was there because "Hitler did not win." This is something that I will never forget and the experience made me feel even closer to him. I am endlessly thankful that I had this opportunity.

Being his only granddaughter, Papa and I have always had a very special bond. Whether it is visiting him at his office or spending time together in Florida, we never fail to have great conversations, many laughs, and lots of hugs. He is a true role model of how to live life in such a positive way. Whenever I am told that I remind someone of Papa, I consider it the greatest compliment. I am the luckiest granddaughter to have such an incredible person as my papa!

ALEXANDRIA NEWMAN'S TRIBUTE

As a teacher, I have often asked my students to write about their hero. Mine is an easy choice: my dad. He is an extraordinary father and papa. My hero is loving, hard-working, kind, funny, and warm. I have watched my dad with great admiration for how hard he works and how much love he gives. Even though he often still works six days a week at his office and prefers not to take a vacation, he always takes my calls. He is a snazzy dresser, and I smile when I think of him in jeans for the first (and last) time at the age of eighty. My dad is kind to everyone and it is no surprise that his family and friends adore him. There is a funny side to my dad as well. He good-naturedly let me put curlers in his hair when I was young and always kept me busy at synagogue by tying the ribbon from the middle of a prayer book around my finger. My dad likes nice restaurants with tablecloths, yet one of his secret pleasures is a small McDonald's hamburger and fries with no salt.

My dad radiates warmth from his smile and his eyes. He frequently sings and dances with my sons and plays the best pretend piano at the dinner table. Recently, I've been hearing him sing songs in Czech. He loves to see his family, and at times I notice him a little emotional when we leave after a visit. Without exception, he watches me drive down the driveway to blow a kiss or give the peace sign and I honk my horn and blow kisses back. Many friends, not just family, affectionately refer to him as Papa. For as long as I can remember, my nickname for him has been Papa Smurf.

I treasure the time we spend together. Some of my very favourite times with my dad have been when we meet for coffee on the weekends. I hope he knows that there is nowhere I would rather be at those times than right there with him. We speak daily; he wants to check in on me and his grandchildren. My dad does so much for his family and the only thing he wants in return is for us to be happy. He is the strongest, and yet most gentle, man I know. My dad is my hero because of the kind of man he is. He is a loving, constant role model for my boys and I couldn't love him more!

JARED ROTHBLOTT'S TRIBUTE

The most memorable moments with Papa are the understated ones. He'll be sitting at the head of his dining room table while the family converses during a meal. Possessing a quiet, peaceful demeanour, a proud father and grandfather observes his family. At every gathering, a moment occurs where I, too, grow quiet, just soaking in the conversation. At some point, I look at Papa. His eyes find mine, smiles grow upon our faces, and we nod our heads. Without a single word, we understand each other. To him, seeing his family happy, healthy, and together is pure bliss. For someone who survived a horrific adolescence and was thrown into the world with a mere $10 in his pocket, the life he's built for himself and our family is truly remarkable. I'm proud of my grandfather, my role model, my friend.

HARRISON ROTHBLOTT'S TRIBUTE

When I was in high school, I performed in a play called *Cabaret*, set in Weimar, Germany, just as Nazism was on the rise. I was aware that my papa had suffered through the Holocaust and even told him that I'd understand if he didn't come to see the play, but he was adamant that he wanted to see my performance. A week or so after the show closed, I nervously sat down with my papa to get his thoughts about the play. He paused and then began to speak. "It was hard, very hard, to watch that, but it is important. It is better to remember than to forget what happened." I can still hear his voice saying those words, and his message has stuck with me to this day. It just showed how strong my papa is.

A few months later, my photography teacher told us that we had one more project to turn in before the end of the year and we could create anything that was meaningful to us. That evening I called my papa and proposed my project. I went to his house that weekend and we grabbed boxes from his office and from the basement and went through pages and pages of photo books. As I would joke to Papa, it reminds me of who to thank for my good looks. When we were finished, I had two big bags of photos to scan and digitize once I got home. However, the photographs were only half of the project I had planned.

After performing in *Cabaret*, I had a deeper understanding of how important it was to gather first-person testimony about this era, so I set up a microphone on the kitchen table and recorded my papa's comments as we looked at the photographs. For the first time, he told me about his childhood, his liberation from the camps, and his time on the *Aquitania*, the ship that brought him across the Atlantic to Canada. He talked about his time with his foster family, the Forgangs, and finishing high school at

Bloor Collegiate. We laughed at the photographs of him with lots and lots of different ladies, even some from as far back as his days in Europe after being liberated from the camps.

When it came time to present my project to the class, I put up the images on the big screen, played the audio over the speakers, and the class went silent. They were just as engrossed in hearing him speak about his life as I had been when I was sitting at that dining room table, the moments of laughter and of sadness, and a few moments where my papa was silent. Everyone was there in that moment, and it's a moment I wouldn't trade for anything.

THE LINDYS' TRIBUTE

[The following was written on the eve of Tom's belated ninetieth/ninety-first birthday celebration on July 18, 2021.]

Dear "Uncle Tom":

Mazel Tov on reaching this incredible milestone! Over all the years we've known you, your demeanour, sense of humour, and outlook has never changed. You still have the "glass half full, it's never cloudy, just partly sunny" way of looking at things, and we all look to you as a fantastic role model and some-one we should aspire to emulate. Perhaps that's why you've survived so many of life's challenges. Here you are still driving, working, and enjoying life to its fullest! We all look forward to sharing more milestones and mitzvahs in the future! It's an honour and privilege to share this special time with you.

With much love and sincerity,
Jamie, Laura, Sean & Cory!

DAVID, ELLEN, AND KATE LINDOVER'S TRIBUTE

[The following was written on the eve of Tom's belated ninetieth/ninety-first birthday celebration on July 18, 2021.]

We are so thankful the vaccination drive has made great headway, allowing us the opportunity to celebrate your special birthday. And as we gather together to honour you, it is clear that this is much overdue.

It is your turn to assume the spotlight and be celebrated, with all of your admirers here and elated. As the patriarch of a large and blended family, we are thankful for the countless get-togethers and your generous hospitality.

We admire your calm and patient demeanour, a few lessons we can learn from our humble leader. You have lived your life spreading love and affection, and always made us feel part of a strong family connection. We have enjoyed years of conversations about our days, families, and world events, and always look forward to hearing your insightful "two cents." At times we might even disagree, but the consummate gentleman you are, would always avoid a good spar.

As we celebrate this special milestone birthday with you, we are reminded of all the wonderful qualities you imbue. How lucky we are to have shared so many moments together and look forward to many more now and forever.

Much love,
David, Ellen, and Kate

EVA NEWMAN'S TRIBUTE

Tommy has always encouraged me as an artist and appreciated the work I do. I recall him flying to Calgary for the opening of an exhibition I had in the early 1980s at the Calgary Jewish Community Centre and purchasing a couple of works from that show. More recently, he ordered multiple sets of my cards to use for Season's Greetings cards for his clients. When I was raising money for another exhibition, he stepped up to the plate without a second thought. He often asks if I am still painting and is pleased to hear that I am. I also have very fond memories of going to the symphony with him in Toronto. His appreciation for the arts, both visual and performing, is impressive. When we would go for walks, his gentle soul was equally in tune with the birds, flowers, and overall beauty of the natural world.

In 1974, I moved to Toronto after spending a year in Southeast Asia. Tommy was always there for me, treating me to lunches and dinners and even taking care of my dry cleaning! Once, I remember he took me to one of Jeanette's concerts and I was wearing drawstring, beach-like cotton pants from Malaysia. ("The last of the flower children," Mommy would call me.) Needless to say, Tommy was not impressed, but he loved me nonetheless. As long as I can remember, I have been able to speak openly with Tommy about personal, financial, and political matters. He has always been thoughtful, philosophical, and eternally optimistic. Another outstanding quality of Tommy's is that I have never, in my whole life, ever heard him say anything negative about anyone. Never! He is a true gentleman and a remarkable human being.

It was my father's seventy-fifth birthday in June 1977. Tommy surprised his uncle by arriving and we celebrated in my parents' garden. My father was overjoyed to see Tommy!

I remember him treating Mommy, along with me and my two daughters, Jessica and Annik, to a stay at the very upscale Windsor Arms Hotel when we came for Audrey's wedding. He is always generous, without missing a beat, and humble, so very humble. To this day, his enduring love for me and my family is overwhelmingly important and significant to us all.

JESSICA MOSSIERE'S TRIBUTE

When I think of Tommy, his warmth, kindness, generosity, and modesty are what comes to mind.

He has always included us in the family, even though we live far away. I've always felt so close to our Toronto cousins and that is in great part because of his inclusive nature.

I remember him flying Annik and me to Kelowna several years ago so that we could spend a weekend at Big White with Audrey's family. He didn't need to do that but knew how much it would mean to us. It was really a wonderful weekend.

His focus has always been family. This book is such a beautiful outcome of all the heartache and adversity faced early on in his life.

His will, determination, and work ethic are truly inspiring to me, and to many others, I'm sure. I don't know anyone else who works as hard as he does.

Tommy is truly a gentleman. We are so lucky to be a part of his family, even at a distance.

ANNIK MOSSIERE'S TRIBUTE

The first thing that comes to mind when I think of Tommy and my favorite moments is when we exchange words in Czech. My grandmother taught me my first Czech words and I always try to use all the words I know when talking with Tommy and ask him to teach me new words. I can hear/see him light up and smile when we do this and it makes my heart happy. This activity feels like our own special bond and I so appreciate how Tommy keeps me connected to my Czech roots that way. I've been saying all those Czech words to my son, Thomas, since he was born and hope to pass those on to him.

This brings me to my next thought about Tommy. When choosing a name for our son, we considered many things, including the fondness, love, and respect we have for Tommy and how special and meaningful it would be for our son to have that name and connection to Tommy forever. We had the name in mind but didn't know for sure what name we would officially pick until the day he was born. The second we lay eyes on him, we both knew it had to be Thomas. We did know that if we had a boy, the middle name would be Arthur, and it just seems so fitting and special to have "Thomas Arthur" together.

My heart was overloaded with love when we came to Toronto in January 2020 and Tommy had the chance to meet Thomas. "Little Thomas" and "Big Thomas" together! They seemed to immediately have a special bond and it brought me to tears watching them look into each other's eyes with such genuine love and curiosity. I'll never forget that visit. We've printed a big picture of them looking at each other, and have it put up across from Thomas's crib. He looks up and sees it every day, pointing and smiling, and asking to see it up close.

As a kid, I always looked forward to Toronto visits to see the family. I can't remember specific memories, but more a general feeling of peace, connection, and inclusion. Tommy has always been so gentle, kind, and generous. He's a charmer and he smiles with his soul—seeing his eyes light up during family visits has always made me know we are special to him and him to us.

CHUCK (KAREL) NEWMAN'S TRIBUTE

It would be easy, when asked about their memories of Tom, for people to simply list the many things that he did for them. There is no question that this urbane, generous, and caring man always displays a keen interest in others and asks for nothing in return. Tom is a primary role model not only to me but to his family, friends, and business associates.

But consider what intelligence and strength of character it takes for someone to lose everything, and nearly everyone, as a teenager, survive the worst of a war, move to a new country, learn a new language, train in a challenging profession, and successfully build and maintain his own business. Tom manages to keep a sense of humour, remains consistently even-tempered, and demonstrates a lack of harsh judgments in nearly all situations. He is reliable to his family and those he deals with socially and in business. And consider the determination it takes for someone to keep working on a daily basis, long after his contemporaries have taken their leave.

My earliest memories of Tom may come from post-war street photos of us taken in Prague. In them, I was perhaps three or four years of age; he was fifteen or sixteen. They show a smiling young man, whom I came to regard as my older brother. It is my hope that when I reach his age, I will be moving along the same path he is on. Tommy is a very good man.

RHYS NEWMAN'S TRIBUTE

After reminiscing, what stands out to me is how much my dad, Chuck (Tom's first cousin), and Tom are alike. It's not possible to accurately distill, but their compass seems to point in a direction something like this: "Success is to humbly achieve with integrity."

There are so many memories, but here are a couple of gems. One day, we all went to see Harrison perform in a play. At the end, as we were all preparing to leave, Tommy smiled and started dancing like no one was watching. It was noon on a weekend at a high school, but as far as he was concerned, it could have been a Broadway stage.

The other time was when Kristina and I were at dinner at Audrey and Graham's. Tom managed to get me to sit down next to him, gave me that "Tom Stare," and asked me what my plans were with Kristina. I told him, in confidence, that I was going to propose to her, but I emphasized that it was a secret. He patted my shoulder, said how happy he was for us, and shouted, "Kristina, come here, I have something very important to tell you." I gasped as Kristina walked toward him. Tom glanced at me, winked, and whispered, "I'm kidding," and paid Kristina some wonderful compliment proving that, at eighty-nine, he was still more clever than any of us.

MANNY WEISS'S TRIBUTE

"Remember, you have a cousin, Thomas Newman, in Toronto. We call him Shimon." For some reason my mother, Ruth Ecker Weiss, would repeat this to me. Checking with my oldest sister, Doris, she recalls Mom saying this as well. I grew up knowing my cousin Alex Ecker and thinking he was the only survivor of the Shoah in our family.

Assigned to search for cousins for our first reunion in 2009, I recalled what my mother said and contacted Tom. There was no need for an introduction. The love between us was immediate. His kind and gentle nature was just like all the Eckers I know.

My fondest remembrance was at this first reunion. Tom was introduced to about fifty cousins here in the US. He seemed to reach out to each of us, making the connection to an extended family he thought he had lost in the Shoah. Tom had found descendants of his uncle Max Ecker, who made it to the US before World War I. It was a magical moment for Tom and all of us.

Personally, I feel a true love for a man I had only heard about growing up. When he and I meet, whether in Chicago, Colorado Springs, Pennsylvania, Boston, or Toronto, there is a bond that is unshakeable between us. I thank my mother, who is responsible for our meeting. And I thank Tom for coming back to the family with joy and enthusiasm.

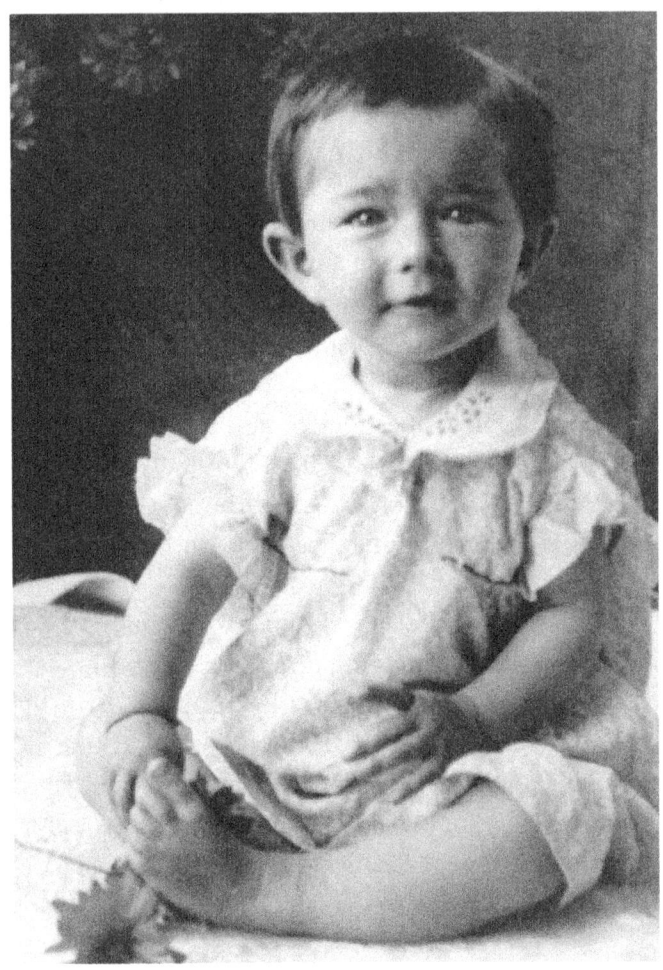

POSTSCRIPT

Life works in mysterious ways... just as I published my memoir and expressed my wish for a photo of my immediate family, a maternal cousin of mine, Lenore Levine (née Ecker), sent me this print of my beautiful little sister Friderika. She is pictured here on August 10, 1934, at the age of nine months. I will treasure this—the only photo I have of anyone in my family—forever.

ACKNOWLEDGMENTS

To Grace, for always being by my side.

To my children, Audrey and Alexandria; my son-in-law, Graham; and my grandchildren, Blake, Cole, Madison, Jared, and Harrison, for your endless love. This is my gift of life to you, and your children, and your children's children.

To Audrey, for your inspiration and tireless determination in making my memoir a reality.

To Alexandria, for sharing my story with your students.

May this be a lesson in positivity and may you all never forget.

To David Hayes, for assisting me in this process with unwavering compassion.

To Jesse, Rony, Nadine, and Jennifer at Page Two for your sensitivity, guidance, and creativity.

To Markus Wegewitz at the Buchenwald Foundation for your generous research assistance.

To all my fellow survivors who have shared their stories and leave legacies for the world to never forget.

LISTS OF
FAMILY
MEMBERS

CURRENT

My current immediate family:

My love, Grace Lindover.

My eldest daughter, Audrey; son-in-law Graham; grandchildren Blake, Cole, and Madison.

My daughter Alexandria; grandsons Jared and Harrison.

Jamie (Grace's eldest son) and Laura; sons Sean and Cory.

David (Grace's son) and Ellen; daughter, Kate; David's children Rachel and Ben.

PATERNAL*

*Note: Not a full representation of the entire paternal side of my family.

Alexander Neumann's side of the family (based on the information that I have):

Grandparents: Jakub Neumann (born 1855, Zamutov, Slovakia) and Anna (Hanna) Friedman (born 1857, Vranov, Slovakia).

Four of my father's siblings immigrated to the United States prior to the war (all originally from the village of Zamutov, Slovakia).

My parents, Alexander Neumann and Rosalia (Ecker), both died in Auschwitz. My siblings Isaac, Artur, Friderika, Ludmila, Irena, and Morris all perished in the camps.

Seren was married and had two sons and two daughters (all perished in the Holocaust).

Rosa (died in an accident).

Karolina (Linka) (born March 10, 1895, in Zamutov; died in Auschwitz in June of 1942) was married to Avrum Lefkowich (died). They had a son, Ernest Lefton, who survived.

Artur Eliaš (Bobek) married Marketa (Gretka); they survived and returned to Prague—I lived with them after the war before going to Canada. They had two children, Charles (Chuck) and Eva. Chuck married Diane, and they had a son named Rhys. Eva has daughters, Jessica and Annik.

Dezsö (David) married Ilona; they survived the war but lost their daughter. I lived with them first, in Budapest, post-war.

Simon survived and lived in Budapest. His son, Zoltan, went to Israel, and his daughter, Ibola, remained in Budapest.

MATERNAL*

* Note: Not a full representation of the entire maternal side of my family.

Rosalia Ecker's side of the family (based on the information that I have):

Yitzak Ecker (grandfather) died in the Holocaust along with my grandmother.

My mother, Rosalia Ecker, married my father, Alexander Neumann, and had seven children: Isaac, Artur, Simon (me), Friderika, Ludmila, Irena, and Morris. I am the sole survivor of my family.

Aaron Ecker married Kate; they lived in the United States before the war, along with their children, Irving and Moishe.

Jonas Ecker married Sarah Brown; they also went to the United States before the war. They had children: Louie, Joe, and Felix.

Jenny Ecker married David Davis; they too moved to the United States before the war. They had children: Phillip, Frances, Irving, and Ruth.

Yetta Ecker was also in the United States.

Yankel (Jacob) Ecker married Rose. Children (names to the best of my knowledge): Fagel, Izak, Rudolf, Reuven, Villiam, and Alex. We lived in the same house together in Vojnatina. Alex, like me, is the sole survivor of his family. Alex and his late wife, Marilyn, had two daughters, Ruth and Francine (husband Azael). Ruth and her husband, Jerry Saul, have two daughters, Jacqueline and Melissa, who each have young children. Alex lives in New Jersey with his family.

Stephen Ecker emigrated to the United States before the war.

Yoho Ecker also moved to the States pre-war.

Max Ecker married Margaret Velkovitz; they went to the United States before the war. They had children: Morris (wife Rose; children Sidney and Howard), Phillip (wife Elsye; sons Larry and Lee), Joseph, Ruth (husband Jack Weiss; children Doris, Lenore, and Manny), Harry (wife Pauline; son Alan), Abraham, and Ethel.

APPENDIX

FIGURE 1.1

Simon Neumann: Cover document

"Buchenwald, Men, Admin number 481971."

"Neumann, Simon."

"Birthdate: 6.4.1930; Birthplace: Vojnatina; Buchenwald
Prisoner number: 123418."

The checklist indicated that six documents are included:

"Personal effects form"

"Entry form"

"Area entry card"

"Medical form"

"Work card"

"Number card"

FIGURE 1.2

Simon Neumann: Personal effects form

"Hungarian Jew; Auschwitz number A6837, Buchenwald number 123418."

"Occupation: Student; Birthdate: 6.4.1930 in Vojnatina."

"Arrival date at Buchenwald: 26.1.45 from Auschwitz."

Stamped words: "No personal effects transferred."

"Certified" followed by the supposed signature of Simon Neumann.

"Signed by personal effects manager" followed by a German signature
which also appears on Artur's card.

FIGURE 1.1

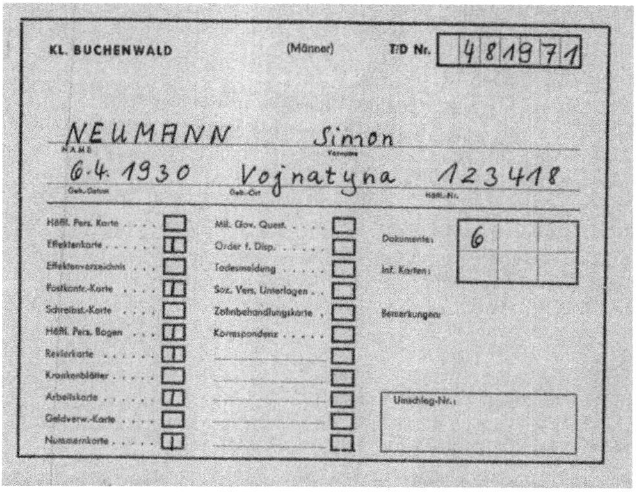

KL. BUCHENWALD (Männer) T/D Nr. 481971

NEUMANN Simon
NAME Vorname

6.4.1930 Vojnatyna 123418
Geb.-Datum Geb.-Ort Häftl.-Nr.

Häftl. Pers. Karte
Effektenkarte
Effektenverzeichnis
Postkontr.-Karte
Schreibst.-Karte
Häftl. Pers. Bogen
Revierkarte
Krankenblätter
Arbeitskarte
Geldverw.-Karte
Nummernkarte

Mil. Gov. Quest.
Order f. Disp.
Todesmeldung
Soz. Vers. Unterlagen
Zahnbehandlungskarte
Korrespondenz

Dokumente: 6
Inf. Karten:
Bemerkungen:
Umschlag-Nr.:

FIGURE 1.2

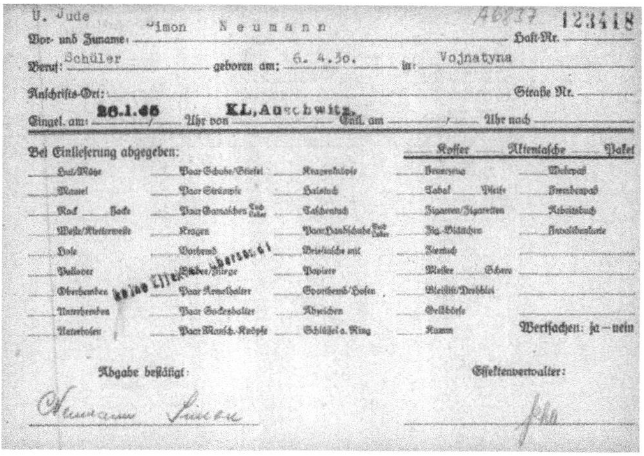

U. Jude
Vor- und Zuname: Simon Neumann Haft-Nr. 46837 123418
Beruf: Schüler geboren am: 6. 4.30. in: Vojnatyna
Anschrifts-Ort: Straße Nr.
Eingel. am: 26.1.45 Uhr von KL, Auschwitz Entl. am Uhr nach

Bei Einlieferung abgegeben: Koffer Aktentasche Paket

Hut/Mütze, Mantel, Rock, Jacke, Weste/Kletterweste, Hose, Pullover, Oberhemden, Unterhemden, Unterhosen
Paar Schuhe/Stiefel, Paar Strümpfe, Paar Gamaschen, Kragen, Vorhemd, Binder/Fliege, Paar Ärmelhalter, Paar Sockenhalter, Paar Mansch.-Knöpfe
Kragenknöpfe, Halstuch, Taschentuch, Paar Handschuhe, Brieftasche mit, Papiere, Sporthemd/Hosen, Abzeichen, Schlüssel a. Ring
Feuerzeug, Tabak, Pfeife, Zigarren/Zigaretten, Zig.-Blättchen, Ziertuch, Messer, Schere, Bleistift/Drehblei, Geldbörse, Kamm
Wehrpaß, Fremdenpaß, Arbeitsbuch, Invalidenkarte
Wertsachen: ja — nein

Abgabe bestätigt:
Effektenverwalter:

FIGURE 1.3
Simon Neumann: Entry form
"Concentration camp; Hungarian Jew; Auschwitz number A6837; Youth;
Buchenwald number 123418."
"Neumann, Simon."
"Birthdate: 6.4.1930 in Vojnatina, Communistic Hungary."
"Occupation: Student; Religion: Of Jewish Religion."
"Citizenship: Hungarian; Status: single."
"Name of father: Sandor, farmer."
"Name of mother: Rosa, born Ecker."
"Name of spouse: No family."
Stamp indicates arrival date from Auschwitz as 26.1.45.
Beneath the stamp there is a form recording body measurements:
"12/24/3" (unknown specifications).

FIGURE 1.4
Simon Neumann: Area entry card
Handwritten number at top right indicates placement in Barrack 57.
"Political Hungarian Jew; Buchenwald number 123418."
"Birthdate: 6.4.1930 in Vojnatina."
"Student."
"Arrival from Auschwitz on 26.1.45."

FIGURE 1.3

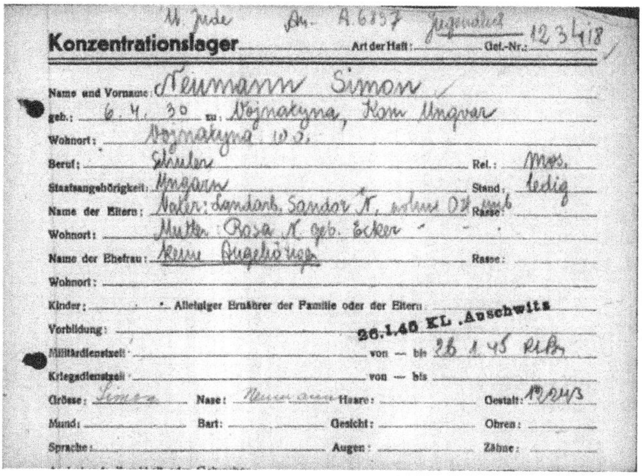
U. Jude Sch. A.6137 Jugendlich

Konzentrationslager .... Art der Haft: .... Gef.-Nr.: 123418

Name und Vorname: Neumann Simon

geb.: 6.4.30 zu: Vojnatyna, Kom Ungvar

Wohnort: Vojnatyna

Beruf: Schüler Rel.: mos.

Staatsangehörigkeit: Ungarn Stand: ledig

Name der Eltern: Vater: Landarb. Sandor N. Rasse:

Wohnort: Mutter: Rosa N. geb. Ecker

Name der Ehefrau: keine Angehörige Rasse:

Wohnort:

Kinder: Alleiniger Ernährer der Familie oder der Eltern:

Vorbildung: 26.1.45 KL. Auschwitz

Militärdienstzeit: von — bis 26.1.45

Kriegsdienstzeit: von — bis

Grösse: Simon Nase: Neumann Haare: Gestalt:

Mund: Bart: Gesicht: Ohren:

Sprache: Augen: Zähne:

FIGURE 1.4

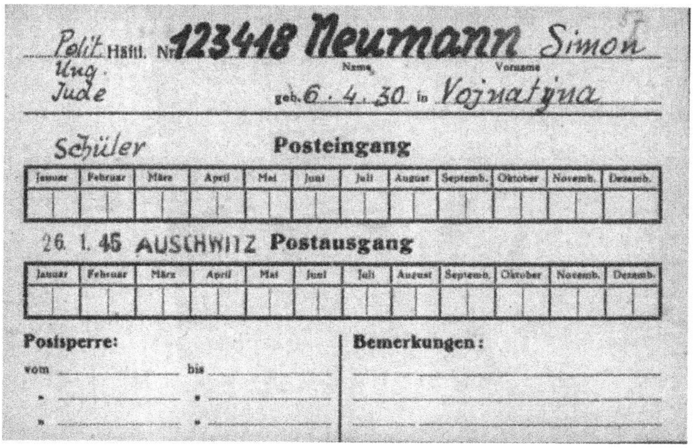
Polit. Häftl. Nr. 123418 Neumann Simon

Name Vorname

Ung. Jude geb. 6.4.30 in Vojnatyna

Schüler Posteingang

Januar	Februar	März	April	Mai	Juni	Juli	August	Septemb.	Oktober	Novemb.	Dezemb.

26.1.45 AUSCHWITZ Postausgang

Januar	Februar	März	April	Mai	Juni	Juli	August	Septemb.	Oktober	Novemb.	Dezemb.

Postsperre:

vom .... bis ....

Bemerkungen:

FIGURE 1.5
Simon Neumann: Medical form

First page, top:
"Political Hungarian Jew."
"Buchenwald number 123418; Neumann, Simon; Birthdate: 6.4.1930 in Vojnatina."
"Arrival date: 26 January 1945; Height: 156 cm; Weight: 40 kg."

First page, left column:
"Medical history and status on entry: Student; Childhood diseases—1945 March, frostbite of both feet."

"Overall body weakness" followed by handwritten numbers indicating physical assessment.

First page, right column:
"Barrack 59"
"Calling in sick."

Second page, left column:
"Findings" with stamped medical abbreviations that indicate a medical procedure or treatment was performed on the date stamped, March 26, 1945.

First page, right column:
Date stamp, followed by a signature. The right-side date indicates the discharge from this infirmary on April 17, 1945, into the care of the makeshift hospital set up by the Americans.

FIGURE 1.5

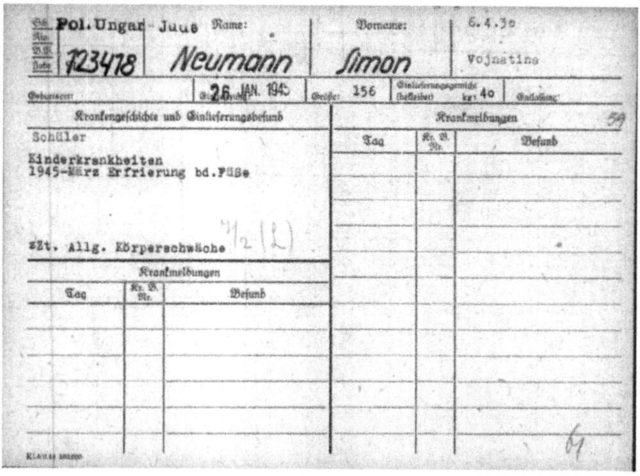

Pol. Ungar Jude Name: Vorname: 6.4.30
123478 Neumann Simon Vojnatina
Geburtsort: 26. JAN. 1945 Größe: 156 Einlieferungsgewicht (bekleidet) kg: 40 Entlassung:

Krankengeschichte und Einlieferungsbefund

Schüler

Kinderkrankheiten
1945-März Erfrierung bd. Füße

zZt. Allg. Körperschwäche 7/2 (2)

Krankmeldungen

Tag	Kr. B. Nr.	Befund

Krankmeldungen 59

Tag	Kr. B. Nr.	Befund

61

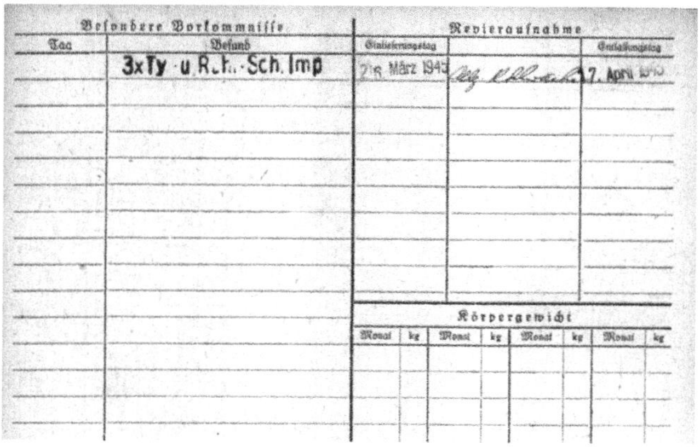

Besondere Vorkommnisse

Tag	Befund
	3xTy · u. R. f. · Sch. Imp

Revieraufnahme

Einlieferungstag		Entlassungstag
2? März 1945	[illegible]	7. April 1945

Körpergewicht

Monat	kg	Monat	kg	Monat	kg	Monat	kg

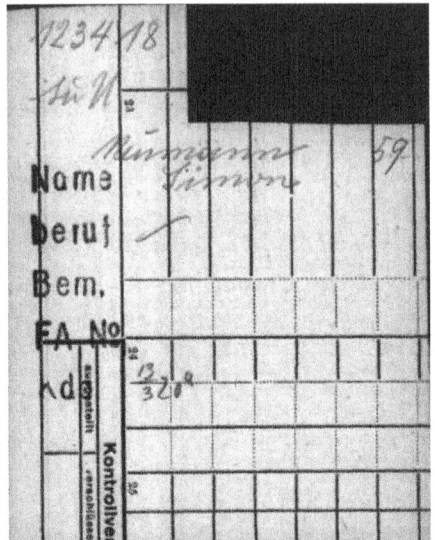

FIGURE 1.6

FIGURE 1.7

FIGURE 2.1

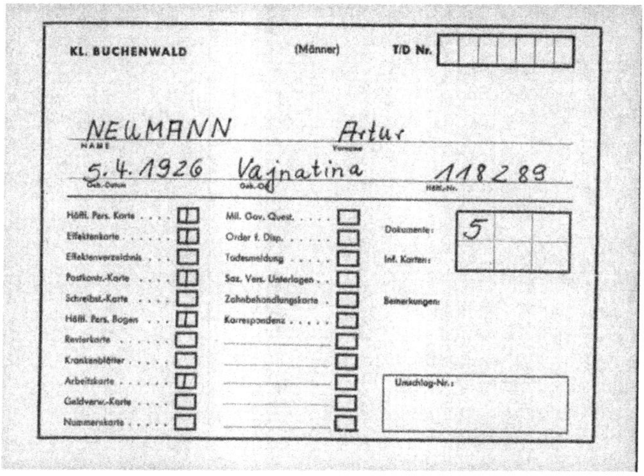

KL. BUCHENWALD (Männer) T/D Nr.

NEUMANN — Name
Artur — Vorname
5.4.1926 — Geb.-Datum
Vajnatina — Geb.-Ort
118289 — Häftl.-Nr.

Häftl. Pers. Karte
Effektenkarte
Effektenverzeichnis
Postkontr.-Karte
Schreibst.-Karte
Häftl. Pers. Bogen
Revierkarte
Krankenblätter
Arbeitskarte
Geldverw.-Karte
Nummernkarte

Mil. Gov. Quest.
Order f. Disp.
Todesmeldung
Soz. Vers. Unterlagen
Zahnbehandlungskarte
Korrespondenz

Dokumente: 5
Inf. Karten:
Bemerkungen:
Umschlag-Nr.:

FIGURE 1.6
Simon Neumann: Work card
"Buchenwald number 123418; Neumann, Simon."
Occupation has a dash, indicating not listed.
Handwritten number indicated on top right corner indicated Barrack 59.
Numbers written on bottom half are the results of an assessment of physical strength.

FIGURE 1.7
Simon Neumann: Number card
"Entry; Admitted; Dismissed." [Blank]
"Buchenwald number 123418; Neumann, Simon. Birthdate: 6.4.1930."

FIGURE 2.1
Artur Neumann: Cover document
"Buchenwald, Men, Admin number [none]."
"Neumann, Artur."
"Birthdate: 5.4.1926; Birthplace: Vojnatina; Buchenwald Prisoner number: 118289."

The checklist indicated that five documents are included:
"Inmate form"
"Personal effects form"
"Entry form"
"Area entry card"
"Work card"

FIGURE 2.2
Artur Neumann: Inmate form

First page
"Concentration camp: Weimar, Buchenwald; Jew."
Triangle symbol with U inside indicated Artur as a Hungarian political prisoner.

First page, left column:
"Neumann, Artur."
"Birthdate: 5.4.1926 in Vojnatina."
"Status: Single."
"Birthplace: Vojnatina, Communistic Hungary."
"Street number: Number 7."
"Religion: Of Jewish religion."
"Relatives: "Father, Sandor, N. residence."
"Admitted: June 1944."
"In concentration camp: Auschwitz."
"Reason: Political Hungarian Jew."

First page, middle column:
"Transferred to Buchenwald: 22.1.1945"

First page, right column:
[Blank]

Second page
"Learned profession: Hair dresser."

FIGURE 2.2

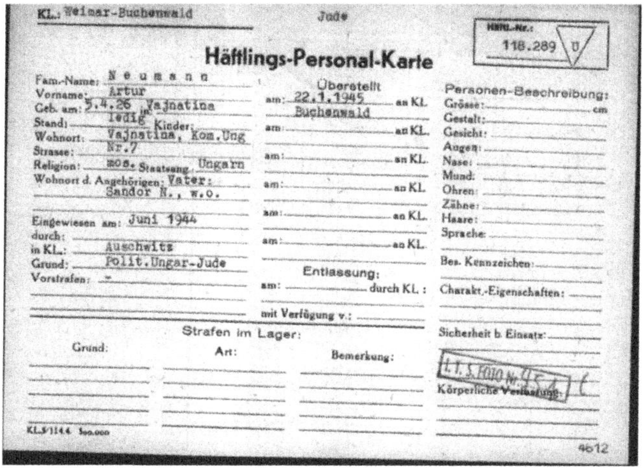
KL.: Weimar-Buchenwald

Jude

Häftl.-Nr.: 118.289 U

Häftlings-Personal-Karte

Fam.-Name: Neumann
Vorname: Artur
Geb. am: 5.4.26 in: Vajnatina
Stand: ledig Kinder:
Wohnort: Vajnatina, Kom.Ung
Strasse: Nr.7
Religion: mos. Staatsang.: Ungarn
Wohnort d. Angehörigen: Vater: Sandor N., w.o.

Eingewiesen am: Juni 1944
durch:
in KL.: Auschwitz
Grund: Polit.Ungar-Jude
Vorstrafen: -

Überstellt
am: 22.1.1945 an KL. Buchenwald
am: an KL.
am: an KL.
am: an KL.
am: an KL.
am: an KL.

Entlassung:
am: durch KL.:
mit Verfügung v.:

Personen-Beschreibung:
Grösse: cm
Gestalt:
Gesicht:
Augen:
Nase:
Mund:
Ohren:
Zähne:
Haare:
Sprache:
Bes. Kennzeichen:
Charakt.-Eigenschaften:
Sicherheit b. Einsatz:
Körperliche Verfassung:

Strafen im Lager:
Grund: Art: Bemerkung:

KL.5/11.44 500.000

4612

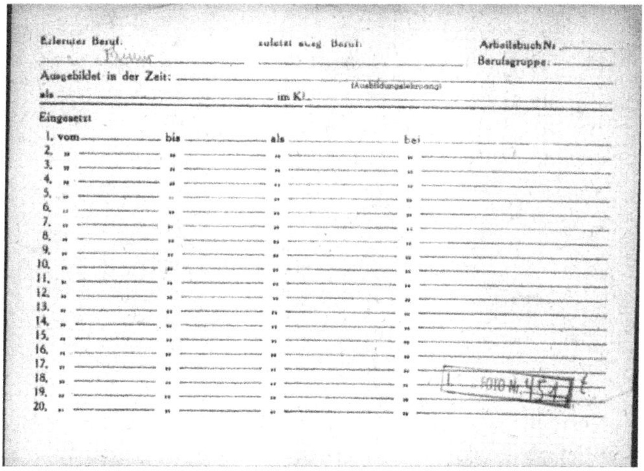
Erlernter Beruf:
zuletzt ausg. Beruf:
Arbeitsbuch Nr.
Berufsgruppe:
Ausgebildet in der Zeit:
(Ausbildungslehrgang)
als im KL.

Eingesetzt
1. vom bis als bei
2. " " " "
3. " " " "
4. " " " "
5. " " " "
6. " " " "
7. " " " "
8. " " " "
9. " " " "
10. " " " "
11. " " " "
12. " " " "
13. " " " "
14. " " " "
15. " " " "
16. " " " "
17. " " " "
18. " " " "
19. " " " "
20. " " " "

FIGURE 2.3
Artur Neumann: Personal effects form
"Hungarian Jew; Artur Neumann; Auschwitz number A7629, Buchenwald number 118289."
"Occupation: Hair dresser; Birthdate: 5.4.1926 in Vojnatina."
"Arrival date at Buchenwald: 22.1.45 from Auschwitz."
Stamped words: "No personal effects transferred."
"Certified" followed by the supposed signature of Artur Neumann.
"Signed by personal effects manager" followed by a German signature.
The same signature appears for both brothers' forms.

FIGURE 2.4
Artur Neumann: Entry form
"Concentration camp; Buchenwald number 118289."
"Neumann, Artur."
"Birthdate: 5.4.1926 in Vojnatina, Communistic Hungary."
"Residence: Vojnatina, Number 7."
"Occupation: Hair dresser; Religion: Of Jewish Religion."
"Citizenship: Hungarian; Status: single."
"Name of father: Sandor, merchant."
"Name of mother: Regina N. [incorrect], born Ecker."
"Name of spouse: No family."
Stamp indicates arrival date from Auschwitz as 22.1.45.
"Family provider: Neumann, Artur." May indicate that he was alone in the camp or he was an adult providing for himself.

FIGURE 2.3

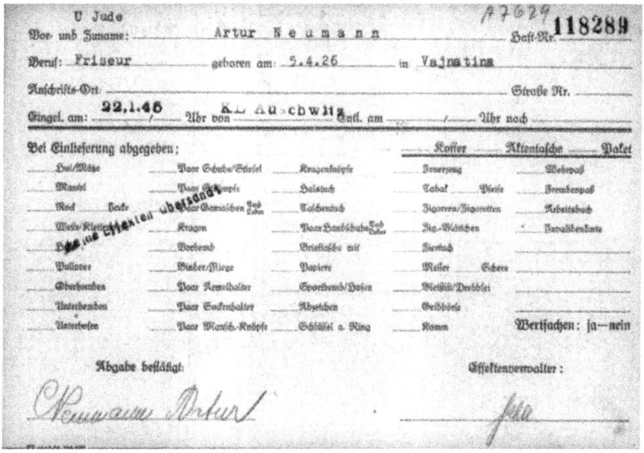

U Jude A7629
Vor- und Zuname: Artur Neumann Haft-Nr. 118289
Beruf: Friseur geboren am: 5.4.26 in Vajnatina
Anschrifts-Ort: Straße Nr.
Eingel. am: 22.1.45 Uhr von KL Auschwitz Entl. am Uhr nach
Bei Einlieferung abgegeben: Koffer Aktentasche Paket
Hut/Mütze Paar Schuhe/Stiefel Kragenknöpfe Feuerzeug Wehrpaß
Mantel Paar Strümpfe Halstuch Tabak Pfeife Fremdenpaß
Rock Hose Paar Gamaschen Taschentuch Zigarren/Zigaretten Arbeitsbuch
Weste Kragen Paar Handschuhe Zig.-Blättchen Invalidenkarte
Vorhemd Brieftasche mit Sacktuch
Pullover Binder/Fliege Papiere Messer Schere
Oberhemden Paar Ärmelhalter Sporthemd/Hosen Bleistift/Drehbleistift
Unterhemden Paar Sockenhalter Abzeichen Geldbörse
Unterhosen Paar Mansch.-Knöpfe Schlüssel a. Ring Kamm Wertsachen: ja—nein
Abgabe bestätigt: Effektenverwalter:
Neumann Artur

FIGURE 2.4

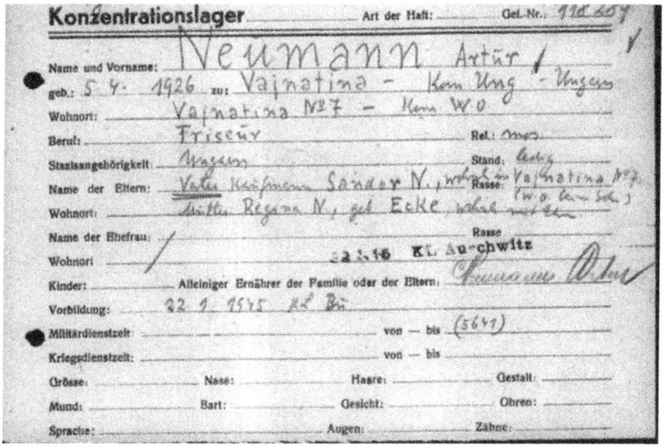

Konzentrationslager Art der Haft: Gef.-Nr.: 118289
Name und Vorname: Neumann Artur
geb.: 5. 4. 1926 zu: Vajnatina – Kom Ung – Ungarn
Wohnort: Vajnatina № 7 – Kom W O
Beruf: Friseur Rel.: mos.
Staatsangehörigkeit: Ungarn Stand: ledig
Name der Eltern: Vater Kaufmann Sandor N., wohnh. in Vajnatina № 7
Wohnort: Mutter Regina N., geb. Ecke
Name der Ehefrau: / Rasse:
Wohnort: / 22.1.45 KL Auschwitz
Kinder: Alleiniger Ernährer der Familie oder der Eltern: Neumann Artur
Vorbildung: 22. 1. 1945 KL Bu
Militärdienstzeit: von — bis (5641)
Kriegsdienstzeit: von — bis
Grösse: Nase: Haare: Gestalt:
Mund: Bart: Gesicht: Ohren:
Sprache: Augen: Zähne:

FIGURE 2.5

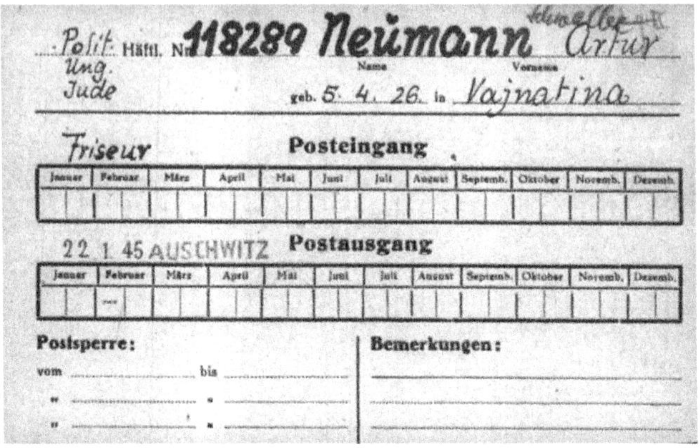
Polit. Häftl. Nr. 118289 Neumann Artur
Ung. Name Vorname
Jude
geb. 5. 4. 26. in Vajnatina

Friseur Posteingang

Januar	Februar	März	April	Mai	Juni	Juli	August	Septemb.	Oktober	Novemb.	Dezemb.

22 1. 45 AUSCHWITZ Postausgang

Januar	Februar	März	April	Mai	Juni	Juli	August	Septemb.	Oktober	Novemb.	Dezemb.

Postsperre:
vom ... bis ...

Bemerkungen:

FIGURE 2.5
Artur Neumann: Area entry card
"Political Hungarian Jew; Buchenwald number 118289."
"Birthdate: 5.4.1926 in Vojnatina."
"Hair dresser."
"Arrival from Auschwitz on 22.1.45."

FIGURE 2.6
Artur Neumann: Work card
"Buchenwald number 118289; Neumann, Artur."
"Occupation: Hair dresser."
Handwritten number indicated on top right corner indicated Barrack 19. Numbers written on bottom half are the results of an assessment of physical strength.

FIGURE 3
Civilian internee card
I was given a Provisional Identification Card as a record of my internment. Though Buchenwald was liberated in April 1945, I spent weeks recovering from the inhuman conditions I had suffered during my internment. I walked out of the hospital on May 16, 1945.

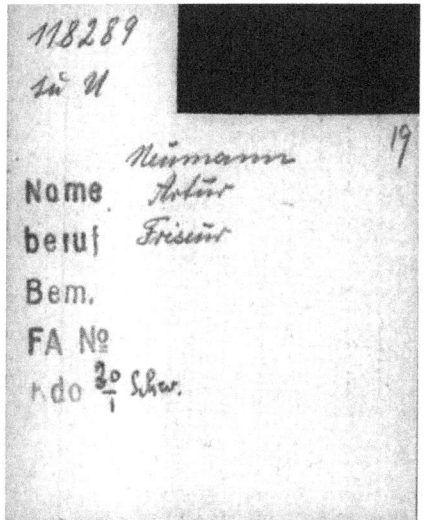

FIGURE 2.6

FIGURE 3

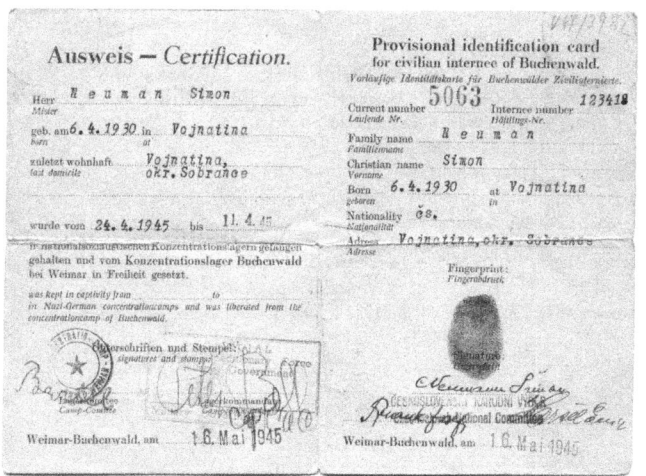

FIGURE 4

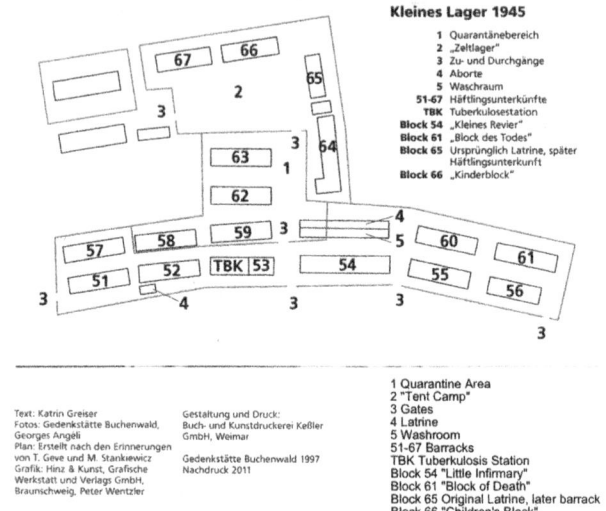

Kleines Lager 1945

1 Quarantänebereich
2 „Zeltlager"
3 Zu- und Durchgänge
4 Aborte
5 Waschraum
51-67 Häftlingsunterkünfte
TBK Tuberkulosestation
Block 54 „Kleines Revier"
Block 61 „Block des Todes"
Block 65 Ursprünglich Latrine, später
Häftlingsunterkunft
Block 66 „Kinderblock"

Text: Katrin Greiser
Fotos: Gedenkstätte Buchenwald,
Georges Angéli
Plan: Erstellt nach den Erinnerungen
von T. Geve und M. Stankiewicz
Grafik: Hinz & Kunst, Grafische
Werkstatt und Verlags GmbH,
Braunschweig, Peter Wentzler

Gestaltung und Druck:
Buch- und Kunstdruckerei Keßler
GmbH, Weimar

Gedenkstätte Buchenwald 1997
Nachdruck 2011

1 Quarantine Area
2 "Tent Camp"
3 Gates
4 Latrine
5 Washroom
51-67 Barracks
TBK Tuberculosis Station
Block 54 "Little Infirmary"
Block 61 "Block of Death"
Block 65 Original Latrine, later barrack
Block 66 "Children's Block"

FIGURE 4
Little Camp

Kleines Lager—also known as "Little Camp"—was a quarantined area in Buchenwald, separated by barbed wire from the main area of the camp. Upon my arrival, I was placed in Barrack 57. At the time, Artur was being held in Barrack 51 for several days before he was moved to Barrack 59. We were in close proximity for four days, a fact I only learned during the research process for my memoir. According to the Arolsen Archives, Artur's fate was "unknown."

Original graphic by Hinz & Kunst Graphische Werkstatt und Verlags GmbH, Braunschweig, Peter Wentzler. Based on the memories of T. Geve and M. Stankiewicz. Gedenkstätte Buchenwald 1997.

FIGURE 5.1

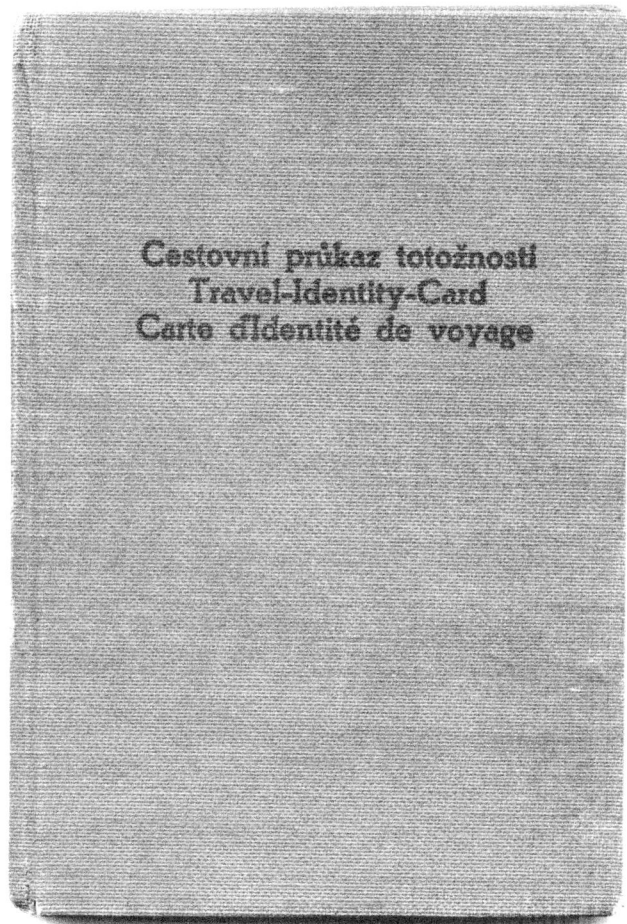

FIGURE 5.1
Czech travel ID (cover)
I received this travel identity card in 1948 from the Ministry of Interior of the Czechoslovak Republic. This ID allowed me to travel within Europe from my temporary home in Czechoslovakia as a person of "uncertain citizenship."

FIGURE 5.1 (inside)

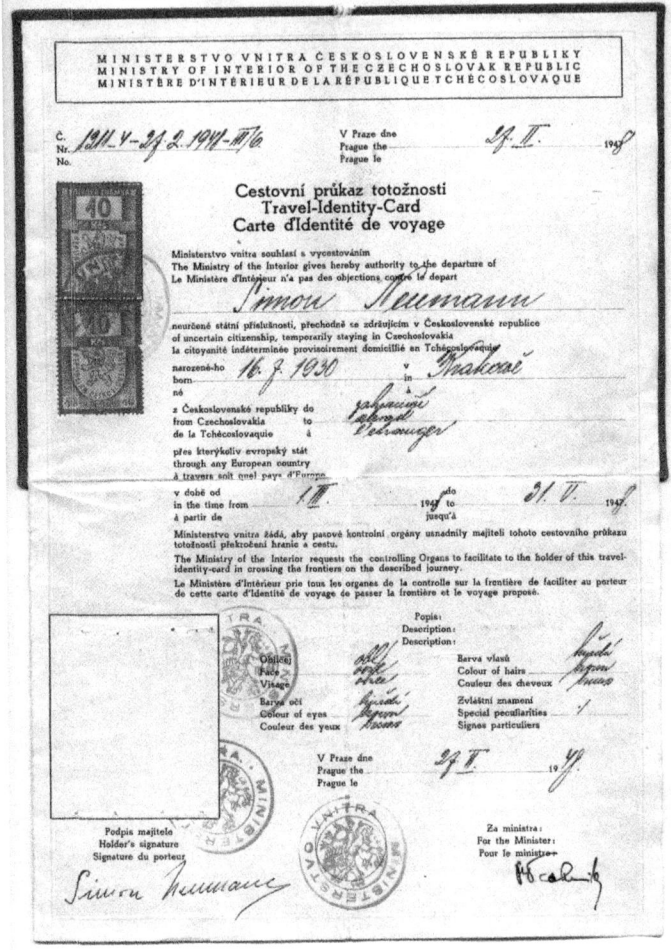

FIGURE 5.1 (inside continued)

FIGURE 6

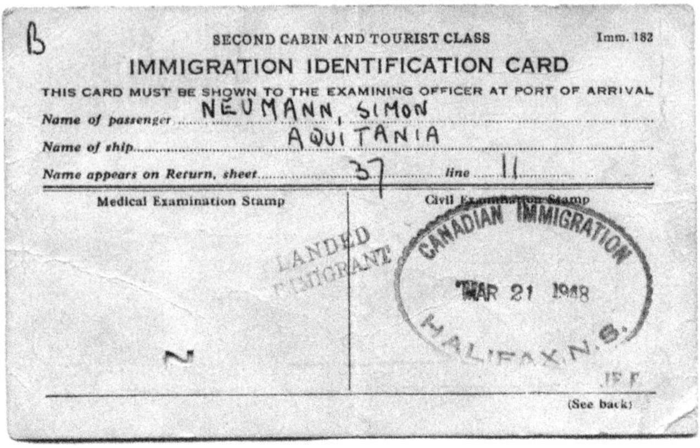
B
SECOND CABIN AND TOURIST CLASS Imm. 182
IMMIGRATION IDENTIFICATION CARD
THIS CARD MUST BE SHOWN TO THE EXAMINING OFFICER AT PORT OF ARRIVAL
Name of passenger NEUMANN, SIMON
Name of ship AQUITANIA
Name appears on Return, sheet 37 line 11
Medical Examination Stamp
Civil Examination Stamp
LANDED IMMIGRANT
CANADIAN IMMIGRATION
MAR 21 1948
HALIFAX, N.S.
(See back)

FIGURE 6
***Aquitania* immigration card**
After several days aboard the RMS *Aquitania*, I received this immigration stamp upon my arrival in Canada at Halifax's Pier 21—known as "Canada's front door"—on March 21, 1948. From 1928 to 1971, Pier 21 heralded the arrival of over one million immigrants.

FIGURE 7.1
Ship log
This is the ship manifest for my journey on the *Aquitania*. The date of departure is March 16, 1948, bound to Halifax, Nova Scotia, Canada. My age is listed as seventeen and my occupation is "Student."

FIGURE 7.2
Ship log (magnified)
Four other War Orphans and I were listed together in the bracket "JEWISH ORPHANS" in transit from Czechoslovakia.

FIGURE 7.1

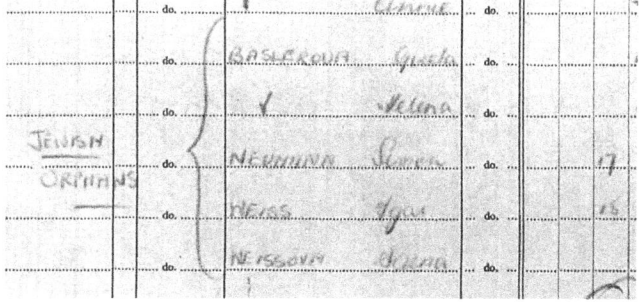

FIGURE 7.2

FIGURE 8

FIGURE 8
Framed recognition document
In May 1996, during a Parliament session held on Holocaust Remembrance Day, Premier of Ontario Michael D. Harris presented recognition documents to eight survivors, including me. Attorney General Charles Harnick said these words: "The sufferings and the testimonies of Holocaust survivors are a song, a hymn of praise, and a testimony to the eternity of the Jewish people and the greatness of their spirit."

RESOURCES AND FURTHER READING

BOOKS, ARTICLES, AND REPORTS

Chamberlin, Brewster, and Marcia Feldman, eds. *The Liberation of the Nazi Concentration Camps 1945: Eyewitness Accounts of the Liberators*. Washington, DC: United States Holocaust Memorial Council, 1987.

Eisen, Max. *By Chance Alone: A Remarkable True Story of Courage and Survival at Auschwitz*. New York: HarperCollins, 2016.

Fraiman, Michael. "A Fresh Start: The Story of Canada's Postwar Jewish Orphans." *Canadian Jewish News*. March 28, 2018. cjnews.com/perspectives/features/the-story-of-1123-orphans-who-came-to-canada-after-the-holocaust.

Frank, Anne. *The Diary of a Young Girl: The Definitive Edition*. Edited by Otto H. Frank and Mirjam Pressler. New York: Bantam Books, 1997.

Krell, Robert. "Child Survivors of the Holocaust—Strategies of Adaptation." *Canadian Journal of Psychiatry* 38, no. 6 (1993). doi.org/10.1177/070674379303800603.

Leipciger, Nate. *The Weight of Freedom*. Toronto: Second Story Press, 2015.

Martz, Fraidie. *Open Your Hearts: The Story of the Jewish War Orphans in Canada*. Montreal: Véhicule Press, 1998.

McManus, John C. "Medics in Hell: Saving the Survivors of Buchenwald." *HistoryNet*. October 2017. historynet.com/medics-in-hell-buchenwald.htm. (Originally published in the October 2017 issue of *World War II* magazine.)

Michlic, Joanna Beata, ed. *Jewish Families in Europe, 1939–Present: History, Representation, and Memory*. Waltham, MA: Brandeis University Press, 2017.

Rosenberg, Albert G., et al. *The Buchenwald Report*. Prepared by a special intelligence team from the Psychological Warfare Division of the Supreme Headquarters Allied Expeditionary Force, assisted by a committee of Buchenwald prisoners (April–May 1945). Translated, edited, and with an introduction by David A. Hackett. Boulder, CO: Westview Press, 1995.

Schmidt, Christine. "Todesmärsche ein Bericht" [Death marches: a report]. In Wolfgang Benz and Barbara Distel (ed.), *Der Ort des Terrors: Geschichte der nationalsozialistischen Konzentrationslager* [Place of terror: a history of the Nazi concentration camps], vol. 3: *Sachsenhausen, Buchenwald* (München: C.H. Beck, 2006), 386–88. (Note: This resource is in German.)

Wiesel, Eli. *Night*. Translated by Marion Wiesel. New York: Hill and Wang, 2006. (The first edition of this book was originally published in 1958 by Les Éditions de Minuit in France.)

ARCHIVES AND ORGANIZATIONS

Alex Dworkin Canadian Jewish Archives: cjarchives.ca/en/c-j-archives/

Arolsen Archives—International Center on Nazi Persecution: arolsen-archives.org/en/

Azrieli Foundation: azrielifoundation.org

Buchenwald and Mittelbau-Dora Memorials Foundation: buchenwald.de/en/580/

Friends of Simon Wiesenthal Center for Holocaust Studies: friendsofsimonwiesenthalcenter.com

Harry S. Truman Library & Museum: trumanlibrary.gov

International March of the Living: motl.org

Neuberger Holocaust Education Centre: holocaustcentre.com

Ontario Jewish Archives, Blankenstein Family Heritage Centre: ontariojewisharchives.org

USC Shoah Foundation: sfi.usc.edu

T OM NEWMAN, a Holocaust survivor, is a chartered accountant with his own firm. He lives in Toronto, where his family also resides. He was an avid tennis player for decades and enjoys the simple pleasures in life. He spends his time doing what he loves most: working in his office and being with his family.

Made in the USA
Monee, IL
07 July 2026

56550200R00173